Reinventing Project-Based Learning

Your Field Guide to Real-World Projects in the Digital Age

Suzie Boss • Jane Krauss

International Society for Technology in Education
EUGENE, OREGON • WASHINGTON, DC

Reinventing Project-Based Learning
Your Field Guide to Real-World Projects in the Digital Age

Suzie Boss • Jane Krauss

Acquisitions Editor: Scott Harter
Production Editor: Lynda Gansel
Production Coordinator: Maddelyn High
Graphic Designer: Signe Landin
Rights and Permissions Administrator: Diane Durrett
Cover and Book Design: Signe Landin
Layout and Production: Newgen–Austin

Library of Congress Cataloging-in-Publication Data

Boss, Suzie.
    Reinventing project-based learning : your field guide to real-world projects in the digital age / Suzie Boss, Jane Krauss. — 1st ed.
        p. cm.
    Includes bibliographical references and index.
    ISBN-13: 978-1-56484-238-1 (pbk.)
    1. Project method in teaching. 2. Internet in education. 3. Educational technology. I. Krauss, Jane. II. Title.
    LB1027.43.B67 2007
    371.3'6—dc22

                                                                          2007038963

First Edition
ISBN: 978-1-56484-238-1

Printed in the United States of America

International Society for Technology in Education (ISTE)
Washington, D.C., Office:
        1710 Rhode Island Ave. NW, Suite 900, Washington, DC 20036-3132
Eugene, Oregon, Office:
        175 West Broadway, Suite 300, Eugene, OR 97401-3003
Order Desk: 1.800.336.5191
Order Fax: 1.541.302.3778
Customer Service: orders@iste.org
Book Publishing: books@iste.org
Book Sales and Marketing: booksmarketing@iste.org
Web: www.iste.org

Cover photo of teacher and student © iStockPhoto.com/marmion

ABOUT ISTE

The International Society for Technology in Education (ISTE) is the trusted source for professional development, knowledge generation, advocacy, and leadership for innovation. A nonprofit membership association, ISTE provides leadership and service to improve teaching, learning, and school leadership by advancing the effective use of technology in PK–12 and teacher education.

Home of the National Educational Technology Standards (NETS), the Center for Applied Research in Educational Technology (CARET), and the National Educational Computing Conference (NECC), ISTE represents more than 85,000 professionals worldwide. We support our members with information, networking opportunities, and guidance as they face the challenge of transforming education. To find out more about these and other ISTE initiatives, visit our Web site at **www.iste.org.**

As part of our mission, ISTE Book Publishing works with experienced educators to develop and produce practical resources for classroom teachers, teacher educators, and technology leaders. Every manuscript we select for publication is carefully peer-reviewed and professionally edited. We look for content that emphasizes the effective use of technology where it can make a difference—increasing the productivity of teachers and administrators; helping students with unique learning styles, abilities, or backgrounds; collecting and using data for decision making at the school and district levels; and creating dynamic, project-based learning environments that engage 21st-century learners. We value your feedback on this book and other ISTE products. E-mail us at **books@iste.org.**

ABOUT THE AUTHORS

Suzie Boss is a journalist who writes about teaching and learning in the 21st century. As a writer and editor at the Northwest Regional Educational Laboratory, she co-authored *Learners, Language, and Technology,* a guidebook focusing on technology to support early literacy. As lead writer for Intel's An Innovation Odyssey project, she interviewed and showcased technology-literate teachers from around the world in daily online features. Boss has also published in *Learning & Leading with Technology, Principal Leadership,* and many other publications. She is a director of the Learning Innovation and Technology Consortium.

A former teacher in Oregon schools, **Jane Krauss** has long been an advocate for technology integration practices in education. As director of Professional Development Services at the International Society for Technology in Education, Krauss traveled internationally, delivering professional development workshops and presentations focused on technology integration. Krauss is chairman of the board of directors of the Learning Innovation and Technology Consortium and has published in *Learning & Leading with Technology.*

ACKNOWLEDGMENTS

Many people contributed to the development of this book.

We are indebted to the many outstanding educators from around the world who have invited our questions and shared their best practices for 21st-century learning. The global educational community is enriched by their experiences.

In particular, we wish to thank Anne Davis and Vicki Davis, two pioneering teachers from Georgia; David Fagg from Australia; international educator Julie Lindsay; Kathy Cassidy, Robert Griffin, and Jeff Whipple from Canada; Pasi Mattila from Finland; Cecilia Magisa Estoque from the Philippines; Linda Hartley from the United Kingdom; Elise Mueller from Washington; Jerome Burg and Esther Wojcicki, both California teachers and members of the Google Teacher Academy; and Adam Kinory of the School of the Future in New York. Thanks, too, to Chris Walsh at WestEd and the Google Teacher Academy.

Several schools opened their doors for site visits and extended interviews. Thanks to Monica Tipton, Carmel Crane, and Michael McDowell from New Technology High School, and Paul Curtis with the New Technology Foundation in Napa, California. Thanks, also, to Kay Graham, principal of the School of IDEAS in Eugene, Oregon, and her teaching colleagues who willingly shared their time, especially Anne Hubbird and Stuart Whitcomb.

In our search for exceptional teachers designing pioneering projects, we were assisted by David Walddon and Kristen Weatherby from the Microsoft Partners in Learning program, host of the Worldwide Innovative Teachers Forum. Thanks to Hilary LaMonte at ISTE who connected us with outstanding teams that were recipients of the Hewlett Packard Technology for Teaching Grants. Matt Dozier of the EAST Initiative provided valuable information about the history and focus of this promising model for 21st-century learning.

Thank you to Glen Bull and his colleagues at the University of Virginia for a stimulating exchange that shaped the conceptualization of "essential learning functions" very early on. Thanks, Tim Lauer, principal and technology wizard, for thoughtful and timely advice. David Barr, thank you for shedding light on the ISTE technology standards development process as it unfolded.

Special thanks to Leslie Conery at ISTE for her unflagging encouragement, and to Steve Burt, technology scout and veteran educator, who shared his considerable expertise about emerging technologies and their potential for the classroom. Thanks to Will Richardson, edublogger extraordinaire, for his encouraging words.

Finally, we thank our families for their patience and support as we dove deeply into this project.

CONTENTS

Foreword by Leslie Conery   ix

SECTION I   ANTICIPATION

Introduction   "I'll Never Go Back"   3

Chapter 1   Mapping the Journey—Seeing the Big Picture   11

Chapter 2   Creating a Professional Learning Community   25

SECTION II   PACKING UP

Chapter 3   Imagining the Possibilities   43

Chapter 4   Strategies for Discovery   59

Chapter 5   Project Management Strategies for Teachers and Learners   75

SECTION III   NAVIGATING THE LEARNING EXPERIENCE

Chapter 6   Project Launch—Implementation Strategies   95

Chapter 7   A Guiding Hand—Keeping a Project Moving   113

SECTION IV   EXPANDING YOUR CIRCLE

Chapter 8   Building Connections and Branching Out   127

Chapter 9   Making Assessment Meaningful   139

Chapter 10   Celebrating and Reflecting   147

SECTION V   UNPACKING

Chapter 11   Bringing It Home   159

APPENDIXES

Appendix A   Essential Learning with Digital Tools, the Internet,
and Web 2.0   165

Appendix B   National Educational Technology Standards
for Students (NETS•S)   183

Appendix C   Reading Group Guide   187

Appendix D   Bibliography   191

INDEX   195

FOREWORD

At last, a book that pulls together the seemingly unconnected concepts, trends, and strategies facing today's educators. The ideas contained in *Reinventing Project-Based Learning: Your Field Guide to Real-World Projects in the Digital Age* are big ideas, important ideas, transformative ideas. The gift of Jane Krauss and Suzie Boss is that they take these big ideas and guide us through them, making them come alive for the classroom.

In reading this field guide, I thought about the many projects currently underway at ISTE and how this book so vividly illuminates the link between theory and practice. For instance, ISTE recently revised the National Educational Technology Standards (NETS) for students in response to shifts in the learning landscape. We put new emphasis on students developing the skills and knowledge needed for success in today's digital world. The spotlight has moved off the technology, and yet technology is ever-present in the standards—just as it is in the world the reader will explore with this guidebook.

As we move away from a primary focus on the technology to acquiring skills and knowledge using technology, critics may say, "You don't need technology to develop communication skills or many of the other skills now emphasized in the NETS. The standards are no longer about technology." They are right. At least, they are right to a point. The standards are about learning and about how technology resources and tools support and enable that learning.

Similarly, it's possible to carry out a learning project without technology. Project-based learning and developing creativity, innovation, research and information fluency, communication and collaboration skills, and many of the other important abilities found in the NETS standards can be accomplished in school devoid of information and communication technology. But what a richer, more authentic landscape it is when students have access to resources, tools, strategies, and concerns found outside the classroom walls. In example after example, this book shows us the world of possibilities awaiting our students.

Like any good field guide, this book leads the reader on an adventure full of discoveries and insights. It also tells us what to look for so we'll know it when we see it. And it helps us meet other travelers on the same journey. Teachers around the globe share their wisdom and experiences in this book, bringing teaching and learning to life.

I recently read a blogger's musings: "When it feels like you are doing everything yourself, it's nice to be able to feel like you are not really alone in your quest." With this publication, Boss and Krauss provide a guidebook to that place where so many elements of real-world learning come together. We're not alone on our learning quest. As you read this book, I hope you heed the authors' advice to bring your colleagues into the conversation.

Enjoy the learning adventure ahead. You'll meet wonderful people, explore new terrain, and remember that as with all true adventures, the learning and success are in the journey as much as in reaching the destination.

—Leslie S. Conery, Ph.D.

Deputy CEO, International Society for Technology in Education

Section I

Anticipation

What are your expectations as you consider teaching with authentic, technology-rich projects? As you set out on this learning journey, consider what motivates you to try new classroom methods and incorporate technology in new ways. Who will accompany you on this adventure? Section I helps you assess your own readiness for change and suggests how to enhance your experience through collaboration with colleagues.

INTRODUCTION

"I'll Never Go Back"

For years, a high school humanities teacher named Adam Kinory thought he was doing a fine job of incorporating technology into his classroom. As computers became more widely available to his students, he made subtle shifts in assignments and expectations to take advantage of new tools. Word processing enabled students to revise their writing without the tedium of repeat typing. The Internet opened new research opportunities. Graphics software made for more compelling presentations. A class Web site helped Kinory communicate about deadlines.

But looking back on his first decade in the classroom, he can see that those shifts did not make for a fundamental change in teaching or learning. He was merely layering technology onto the teaching methods he had learned a decade earlier. "None of that was a leap," he admits. "I didn't really change what I was doing in the classroom."

The "big leap" happened soon after Kinory gained some hands-on experience using digital media, including video cameras and editing software. That experience, which came about through his participation in the Digital Edge Learning Interchange, got him thinking about the role of multimedia in his classroom. Too often, he had watched his students turn off their critical faculties whenever he showed a movie. In particular, he wanted to better engage all students in his special education inclusion class, especially those who are strong visual or auditory learners.

Now, he began to consider a more active use of film—where students would behave more as directors and critics instead of as passive viewers. After all, many of today's students are already savvy about making their own short films. Some upload their productions to sites like YouTube, or use their cell phones to create videos. Kinory's typical student has a blog and belongs to several social networks. Why not build on this digital fluency to reinvent a project for the high school classroom?

Instead of asking students to write traditional thematic essays about the Scopes Monkey Trial, Kinory had them analyze a selection of film clips from *Inherit the Wind* that bring this era to life. He showed students how to embed digitized film clips directly into their documents, linking visual imagery with their written analysis. The assignment not only deepened their understanding of literary theme, but also helped students to think more critically about media as they learned to analyze elements like lighting and blocking. When he asked students to reflect about the project, Kinory could hear them making stronger connections between what they were learning and their own world. (Kinory, 2003)

Both teacher and students had to navigate new ways of working together as the project unfolded, but it didn't hurt that students saw their teacher trying new approaches and taking risks as a learner. At the end of that first reinvented unit, Kinory received a career first: a letter of thanks from his students. If he needed more convincing that he was on the right track, that did it.

The transformation in Kinory's teaching style has been profound—and permanent. "It's natural now for me to integrate technology. A few years ago, my students were surprised but reacted positively when I started using digital tools. Today, my students would react negatively if I didn't teach this way. I'll never go back," he insists, "to the way I used to teach."

Not every successful project ends with a thank-you note. Nonetheless, there are themes in Kinory's story that echo in classrooms around the world. From California to Australia, from Singapore to rural Montana, more and more educators are making similar shifts. They recognize that digital tools are essential features of the environments in which today's students are living and learning. What's more, these educators see how technology opens opportunities to reinvent projects so that they become more authentically connected to students' lives. When they succeed in designing an effective project, teachers are wise enough to recognize that they are also changed by their students' success.

Kinory has continued to introduce new instructional strategies that meet learners squarely in their world, where he sees technology as "a fundamental building block of their experience." When he teaches about point of view in the short story, for instance, he routinely streams audio clips from National Public Radio shows, such as "This American Life," to illustrate key ideas. Some students are motivated to produce their own podcasts. Three were recently selected as winners in an essay contest sponsored by the NPR show "Selected Shorts." Classmates and even other teachers "are starting to see these students in a new and more positive light," Kinory says. (2007)

This book is about the journey that unfolds when teachers decide to move away from traditional teaching and toward this new vision of instructional design. It's a learning journey—for teacher and student alike. For instance, you may decide to take advantage of digital tools for inquiry, collaboration, and communication to connect learners to one another or even to the world beyond the classroom. This endeavor requires learning about new and emerging technologies. You decide to give up the traditional teacher's role of being the content expert, and that means learning new ways to engage with your students. As a Texas high school teacher named Brandy Avant admitted, "Letting go of the silence was the hardest thing, but I realized we have to let students work together and help each other. Now, I get uncomfortable if my class gets too quiet." She's another who has vowed to "never go back" to her old style of instruction.

This is a journey that involves calculated risks. Many of the teachers you will meet in the chapters to come are like Adam Kinory—willing to try new strategies to meet instructional goals and reflective about wanting to improve their own practice so that all learners will succeed. Like him, many also turn to their colleagues as a "sounding board" for new ideas. He regularly brainstorms with a colleague he has come to trust for "helping me formulate critical questions to think about what I'm doing."

Long before we began writing this book, each of us embarked on our own learning journeys that opened our eyes to new possibilities for digital-age instruction. Jane Krauss has seen her approach to teaching evolve during her 20 years in education. She has been a special and general education teacher, supervisor of preservice educators, curriculum writer, presenter, trainer, and director of professional development. In the elementary classroom, she was an early adopter of project-based learning and experienced the shift in what was possible when technologies became available to make projects more authentic, meaningful, and rigorous. Jane continues to work with educators around the world to explore the potential and promise of education technology. Suzie Boss, a journalist specializing in education, has spent much of the past decade observing effective teachers and learning from them about best practices. She has seen how innovative approaches to instruction can combine with new tools to engage learners and transform communities.

Specifically for this book, we have interviewed and observed dozens of teachers who have found success by reinventing the project approach to better meet the needs of digital-age learners. These educators work in all kinds of environments—some of which are more welcoming than others to new ideas for instruction. The educators come from all around the world, and their examples demonstrate how real-world projects can help diverse learners meet instructional goals in wildly different contexts.

Many of these educators feel like pioneers in reinventing project-based learning to take advantage of the opportunities that digital tools afford. Fortunately, they are also willing to share their insights and discoveries. In fact, many of those we highlight are active bloggers who make a point of sharing their learning journeys online so that others can join the conversation. The growing edublogger community provides teachers with increased opportunities to come together to offer improvements, share strategies and enhancements, and work more collaboratively to develop improved versions of promising projects.

STARTING YOUR JOURNEY

Where are you starting your journey? What has motivated you to consider new strategies for the classroom? Maybe you're an old hand at project-based instruction, but now you want to incorporate new technologies to reach ambitious instructional goals. Maybe you're a newcomer to the profession, looking for authentic project ideas you can't find in a textbook. Perhaps your school is part of an initiative that is making new technologies available. Or perhaps you're an administrator or technology specialist, working with a team of teachers on improving instruction across a grade level or subject area.

We start with no assumptions about your past experiences, your students' ages or backgrounds, or the technology tools you have available. Regardless of your role or background, we assume only that you are open to new ideas—and that you like learning.

As we set out on this journey together, keep in mind the following:

- **Today's students are up to the challenge.** The digital world already reaches every aspect of students' lives. Many schools have not kept pace with the opportunities, but most students are primed to take advantage of these new tools.

- **Projects are worth the effort.** As a teacher, your world *will* change, and for the better. Veteran teachers often talk about how they feel rejuvenated as a result of reinventing projects. Many teachers we interviewed expressed the same idea: "I'm not doing the same old lessons we always did, and I'm excited because I'm learning." Don't be surprised if you become more passionate about teaching after taking this journey.

- **Students live and learn in the real world.** From a student's perspective, there's no substitute for the real world when it comes to generating interest in learning. At the end of the day, would you rather see your students dumping their "work" into the recycling bin, or talking about an authentic project in which they are driving their own learning? One science teacher, for example, compares his students to researchers working in industry and academia. At the end of a project, they may publish a monograph to share their original research or participate in a community symposium about science and ethics. They know that their work *matters.*

- **New contexts encourage the project approach.** New learning contexts set the stage for technology-rich, project-based learning. Teacher teaming, professional learning communities, and interdisciplinary instruction facilitate planning and design. New models for using technology, such as laptop initiatives, expand student access to digital tools. New communities of practice—such as the expanding online community of edubloggers—help good project ideas travel and encourage teachers to reflect on what works. All of these factors help to set the stage for success with the project approach, and we highlight several promising models in the pages that follow. For example, Adam Kinory's small New York public secondary school, the School of the Future in Manhattan, with about 100 students per grade, puts a premium on personalization, interdisciplinary learning, and collaboration. In this kind of setting, innovative instructional approaches and technology integration are not only encouraged, but expected.

HOW TO USE THIS BOOK: TURN IT INTO YOUR OWN PROJECT

Field guides are meant to be taken along on a journey. They help you focus your attention on the details that matter. And so it is with this book. It's designed to help you navigate the fast-changing learning landscape of the digital age.

As you work your way through these chapters, use this book as your own learning project. Write in the margins. Turn down pages where you find ideas you want to borrow. Take time to explore the technologies we highlight. In other words, be an active learner who engages with your environment. That's the kind of learning your students will experience as you begin designing and implementing effective projects.

This book has been designed to support your journey whether you are reading alone or working with a group of colleagues. Either way, we hope you find time to talk with others about what you are thinking and learning. Just as good projects involve teamwork, collaboration yields the best results for professional development. Collaboration can range from professional learning communities—which we encourage, and address in more detail in chapter 2—to more informal conversations. In the coming pages, we suggest many ways to open the door for dialogue, either in person or virtually. In addition, we offer a Reading Group Guide (appendix C) with more questions for discussion.

Just as your students arrive with varying levels of readiness, we understand that readers will have a range of entry points for reinventing project-based learning. Some readers will be more comfortable starting small, while others will be ready to dive into more complex projects, and we offer supports all along that spectrum. We have provided opportunities for you to assess your readiness, make choices, direct your learning, explore new ideas, and reflect on your experiences. Throughout the book, you will encounter suggestions for related reading and prompts that encourage you to pause and reflect. Look for these special features throughout the book:

- **Spotlight:** expanded close-up of a teacher, school, or promising model
- **Your Turn:** suggestion for your own hands-on learning or for a collaborative activity to prompt deeper reflection among colleagues
- **Technology Focus:** expanded information about a promising technology to support your project success
- **Side Trip:** related readings or Web resources worth considering

At journey's end, you can look back and see how far you've come—and decide where in the world you want to travel with your students next.

Here's a quick preview of the topics we will explore together:

SECTION I Anticipation

Chapter 1 Mapping the Journey—Seeing the Big Picture

Assess your readiness to begin teaching with technology-rich, authentic projects.

Technology Focus: Social Bookmarking

Chapter 2 Creating a Professional Learning Community

Engage with colleagues, near or far, to build collaboration into project design and enrich your teaching practices.

Technology Focus: Online Communities

SECTION II Packing Up

Chapter 3 Imagining the Possibilities

Establish the conceptual framework for your project. Why do "big ideas" matter in project design?

Technology Focus: Why Use a Wiki?

Technology Focus: Essential Learning with of Digital Tools, the Internet, and Web 2.0

Chapter 4 Strategies for Discovery

How do you begin designing a project? A guided design process helps, whether you build a project from scratch or adapt an existing project plan to meet your needs.

Technology Focus: Track Assets Online

Chapter 5 Project Management Strategies for Teachers and Learners

Teachers and learners alike benefit from improving their project management skills.

Technology Focus: Project Management with Technology

SECTION III Navigating the Learning Experience

Chapter 6 Project Launch—Implementation Strategies

Get your project off to the right start by generating curiosity and preparing students for the active learning ahead.

Technology Focus: Screencasting

Chapter 7 A Guiding Hand—Keeping a Project Moving

Consider the critical roles of classroom discussions, technology use, and troubleshooting strategies in keeping the project moving forward.

Technology Focus: Podcasting

SECTION IV Expanding Your Circle

Chapter 8 Building Connections and Branching Out

Successful projects may take off in directions you did not anticipate. Imagine the possibilities for extensions and connections.

Technology Focus: Online Collaboration

Chapter 9 Making Assessment Meaningful

Near the end of the project, you put your formal assessment plan to use. With 21st-century projects, teachers are incorporating new approaches to make assessment more meaningful.

Technology Focus: Online Grade Books

Chapter 10 Celebrating and Reflecting

Culminating activities remind learners of where they have been and what they have gained along the way.

Technology Focus: Photo Sharing

SECTION V Unpacking

Chapter 11 Bringing It Home

Build time for reflection and sharing into the project life cycle to make the most of your investment in meaningful curriculum design.

Appendixes

Appendix A Essential Learning with Digital Tools, the Internet, and Web 2.0

Examine a wide array of digital tools through the lens of the essential learning they make possible.

Appendix B ISTE National Educational Technology Standards for Students

The new NETS•S express what students should know and be able to do to learn effectively and live productively in an increasingly digital world.

Appendix C Reading Group Guide

Chapter-by-chapter questions are provided to prompt discussions and encourage reflection about your own practice.

Appendix D Bibliography

Your Turn

Where Are You Starting?

Where are you starting your journey? Why? Think about your own previous experiences with project-based learning. If you have already used the project approach with students, what did you like or dislike? What would you like to learn to do better in the future? Do you have regular opportunities to collaborate with colleagues? Where do you turn first to sound out new ideas for your classroom?

If you already have a blog where you reflect on your teaching practice, use it to capture these thoughts. If you don't, consider setting up a blog now. A blog offers you an ideal space to track your reflections over time. And, as you will see in the chapters ahead, becoming an edublogger will connect you with an online community of educators who share your interests.

Do you need help setting up a blog? Chances are, an experienced blogger is within reach. Consider asking your school or district technology coordinator or media specialist for help. Find out if any of your fellow teachers (or students) are blogging. (For more discussion about blogs, see appendix A: Essential Learning with Digital Tools, the Internet, and Web 2.0.)

CHAPTER 1

Mapping the Journey—
Seeing the Big Picture

Scott Durham, a young teacher, was hired to join the faculty at the same Michigan school where he had once been a student. Before the new year began, Durham took a stroll down the halls. He indulged in a little nostalgia as he wandered past his old classrooms. Then he asked himself a critical question: "What had I actually *done* in those rooms?" He could remember getting good grades on tests and assignments, but he couldn't come up with a single memory about a project that had made him excited about learning. On the spot, he promised himself—and his future students—that he would pursue "teaching in a different way."

Project-based learning—powered by contemporary technologies—is a strategy certain to turn traditional classrooms upside down. When students learn by engaging in real-world projects, nearly every aspect of their experience changes. The teacher's role shifts. He or she is no longer the content expert, doling out information in bite-sized pieces. Student behavior also changes. Instead of following the teacher's lead, learners pursue their own questions to create their own meaning. Even the boundaries of the classroom change. Teachers still design the project as the framework for learning, but students may wind up using technology to access and analyze information from all corners of the globe. Connections among learners and experts can happen in real time. That means new kinds of learning communities can come together to discuss, debate, and exchange ideas.

The phrase "21st-century learning" slipped into use long before the calendar rolled over to 2000. A robust debate about the needs of digital-age learners and the workforce needs of the new century continues to engage a global audience. The business world demands employees who know how to work as a team, access and analyze information, and think creatively to solve problems. In the academic world and the blogosphere, educators routinely call for new strategies to better connect with the plugged-in generation known as the Millennials. But with the new century now well underway, the shift in teaching necessary to realize this vision is far from complete.

You may already be familiar with traditional project-based learning, which has been shown to be effective in increasing student motivation and improving students' problem-solving and higher-order thinking skills (Stites, 1998). In project-based learning, students investigate open-ended questions and apply their knowledge to produce authentic products. Projects typically allow for student choice, setting the stage for active learning and teamwork.

Reinventing the project approach doesn't mean discarding this venerable model. Rather, we advocate building on what we already know is good about project-based learning. By maximizing the use of digital tools to reach essential learning goals, teachers can overcome the boundaries and limitations of the traditional classroom. Some tools open new windows onto student thinking, setting the stage for more productive classroom conversations. Others facilitate the process of drafting and refining, removing obstacles to improvement. Still others allow for instant global connections, redefining the meaning of a learning community. When teachers thoughtfully integrate these tools, the result is like a "turbo boost" that can take project-based learning into a new orbit.

What are the hallmarks of this reinvigorated approach to projects?

- Projects form the centerpiece of the curriculum—they are not an add-on or extra at the end of a "real" unit.

- Students engage in real-world activities and practice the strategies of authentic disciplines.

- Students work collaboratively to solve problems that matter to them.

- Technology is integrated as a tool for discovery, collaboration, and communication, taking learners places they couldn't otherwise go and helping teachers achieve essential learning goals in new ways.

- Increasingly, teachers collaborate to design and implement projects that cross geographic boundaries or even jump time zones.

When these components come together in a successful project, the result is transformative, for both teachers and learners. The young teacher described earlier in this chapter developed an alternative to the textbook-driven approach to teaching history. He teamed up with the media specialist at his school to design a project in which students use online collections from the U.S. Library of Congress to investigate primary source materials. His students now make their own sense of history by analyzing the events and artifacts of the past—just as "real" historians do. It took Durham some time to develop his new instructional strategies, because students had to learn new skills, such as understanding text written in antiquated language. He had to hone his own collaboration skills to effectively plan a project with the media specialist. But the payoff on his investment has been huge. He compares the experience to a weight having been lifted off him. "I've gained such freedom as a teacher knowing that my students are now free to find meaning for themselves," he says.

Individual teachers are not alone in discovering these benefits. Gradually, projects are beginning to take hold across schools, and even across systems, as drivers of school improvement. At New Technology High School in California, the project approach is the cornerstone of instruction for the entire school and has spread to a growing network of schools across the U.S. (See Spotlight: The New Technology Model, page 15.) In Singapore, project-based learning is a national goal. The Ministry of Education in Singapore encourages teachers to adopt the project approach with the motto: "Teach Less, Learn More." In Scotland, teachers are forming a professional community around the idea of Extreme Learning, in which teaching and learning are seen as participatory, collaborative, and creative.

When teachers facilitate well-designed projects that use digital tools, they do much more than create memorable learning experiences. They prepare students to thrive in a world that's certain to continue changing.

Side Trip

Tour the Blogosphere

The growing online community of edubloggers generates lively conversations about the direction education is heading. Listen in, or join the discussions, at the following blogs:

- 2¢ Worth—David Warlick is a veteran teacher, provocative author, and technology advocate. http://davidwarlick.com/2cents

- Cool Cat Teacher—"Teacherpreneur" Vicki Davis blogs about innovations in learning, including her own collaborative, global, online projects. http://coolcatteacher.blogspot.com

- EduBlog Insights—Anne Davis from Georgia State University is an elementary educator and instructional technology advocate who has pioneered the use of blogs with young writers. http://anne.teachesme.com

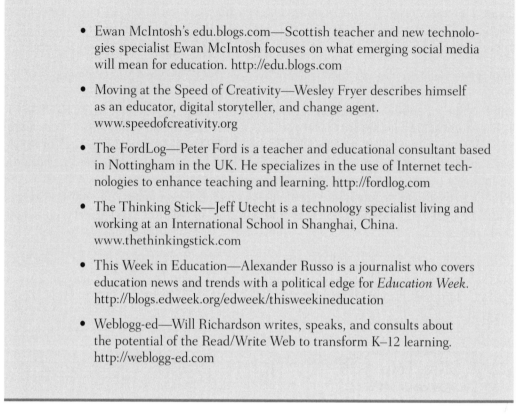

- Ewan McIntosh's edu.blogs.com—Scottish teacher and new technologies specialist Ewan McIntosh focuses on what emerging social media will mean for education. http://edu.blogs.com

- Moving at the Speed of Creativity—Wesley Fryer describes himself as an educator, digital storyteller, and change agent. www.speedofcreativity.org

- The FordLog—Peter Ford is a teacher and educational consultant based in Nottingham in the UK. He specializes in the use of Internet technologies to enhance teaching and learning. http://fordlog.com

- The Thinking Stick—Jeff Utecht is a technology specialist living and working at an International School in Shanghai, China. www.thethinkingstick.com

- This Week in Education—Alexander Russo is a journalist who covers education news and trends with a political edge for *Education Week*. http://blogs.edweek.org/edweek/thisweekineducation

- Weblogg-ed—Will Richardson writes, speaks, and consults about the potential of the Read/Write Web to transform K–12 learning. http://weblogg-ed.com

TEACHERS ARE LEARNERS, TOO

Traditional project-based learning is still a relatively new idea for most teachers. It's not the kind of instruction most of us ever had a chance to experience as students. Bringing digital-age technologies into the picture makes it even less familiar. For teachers who have never observed technology-rich, project-based learning in action, it may be hard to even imagine what a 21st-century project looks like.

Fortunately, as lifelong learners, we all have experiences by which we discover new information and learn to use new tools to achieve our goals. In our daily lives, we tackle all sorts of projects—from building a garden shed to planning a vacation to hosting a dinner party. The learning curve can feel steep the first time around, especially if we have to master a new tool or technology to get the job done. We may run into challenges, discover we need to conduct more research, or seek out expert advice. Then there's that feeling of satisfaction—even celebration—when we reach the goal.

Isn't that the kind of memorable learning experience you want for your students, too?

"The only thing I can remember from my high school biology class is cutting open a frog," says Michael McDowell, a New Technology High teacher who now uses the project approach as the foundation of his curriculum. He sees projects as the best way to help his students master the big ideas of biology. But it's just as important to him that his students gain experience and learn broader skills. "Years from now, I want my current students to remember that my classroom is where they not only learned about biology, but where they also learned how to work as a team how to solve a problem, how to deal with change," he says. "And if they happen to forget the precise definition of mitosis, I want them to be able to know how to find the answer again if they need it."

Spotlight

The New Technology Model

During his first seven years of teaching, Paul Curtis tried valiantly to make project-based learning work in a traditional high school environment. He was convinced that real-world learning offered benefits that textbook-based instruction couldn't match. But despite his enthusiasm, he hit one obstacle after another. "Unless the whole school is convinced this is the way to go, you're fighting this huge uphill battle," he says. "No one else has the students working together in teams. No one else asks students to make presentations or assesses them the way you do. Your class is significantly more rigorous and more challenging, even though you may assign less homework."

Eventually, Curtis left to join the staff of New Technology High, a school designed from the ground up to meet the needs of 21st-century learners. As a farewell gift, Curtis's former colleagues gave him the Don Quixote Award— a recognition of his pursuit of windmills. But for Curtis, the move to New Technology High felt like a homecoming: "I found myself in a place where project-based learning drives the entire curriculum model."

At New Tech, project-based learning is indeed the centerpiece of instructional design. The entire culture of the school supports this approach. Technology is pervasive. Textbooks are scarce. Students have computers within reach at any time, from every classroom. Their "project briefcases" are stored on a server, which they can access from any computer connected to the Web—at home, at school, anywhere, anytime. Collaboration is a given for both students and teachers.

FACING THE FUTURE

New Technology High was founded in Napa, California, in 1996, after local business leaders expressed concern about meeting the workforce needs of the 21st century. They challenged the school district to find a better way of preparing students for the future by having them learn to think critically, collaborate as part of a team, and use technology as a tool for solving problems. In turn, the business community pledged financial support to invest in a cutting-edge infrastructure for learning.

The New Tech model emerged from four years of research and planning. Designers of this forward-thinking school looked widely for promising practices. They surveyed the literature about high school reform. They consulted with experts on professional development and school change. "Everything we do is based on research," explains Monica Tipton, principal of New Tech High since 2006. "We encourage teachers to experiment and innovate, but nothing is frivolous in terms of the research base behind it."

A DESIGN FOR CHANGE

What are the hallmarks of the New Tech model?

- It's small by design, with no more than 100 students per grade in a remodeled building that once housed an elementary school. A maximum student body of 400 allows for greater personalization. Admission is by lottery. In a setting where staff and students get to know one another well, less time gets spent on student management issues. That leaves more time for learning.

- Projects that immerse students in real-world learning are the centerpieces of instruction.

- Technology is everywhere, but it's not the main focus. In this environment, there is always a computer accessible to every student, but technology is consistently viewed as a tool rather than as the focus of learning. "Once you get the hang of it," says a 10th-grader about the many online applications, "you just glide along." Web-based tools allow for collaboration on many levels—between student and teacher, among teachers, and between students and experts outside the school. Students create digital portfolios that encourage them to reflect on their learning over time.

- Teachers are given time and incentives to work together, including shared planning time and staff meetings that focus squarely on instruction. A critical friends approach fosters a culture of collaboration. As Tipton (2006) explains, "Before a teacher introduces a new project to her students, she can ask her peers, 'OK, here's my plan. Now, where are the holes?'"

- Online assessment tools enable teachers to provide students with feedback that goes far beyond a single grade. A student is likely to receive multiple grades on one project, better focusing his or her attention on areas for improvement.

- Good ideas are shared. Designing a new project requires hours of planning on the front end. By developing an online project library, teachers have a place to share completed projects and search for ideas they want to adapt for their own classrooms.

REPLICATION UNDERWAY

Through the New Technology Foundation, established in 2000, key elements of this model are now being replicated across the United States. Support from the Bill & Melinda Gates Foundation has contributed to the expansion. By 2006, the number of sites in the New Tech network had grown to 24. Settings range from urban areas to rural communities, from stand-alone institutions to small schools within larger high schools. Meanwhile, hundreds of visitors from around the world come each year to observe the New Tech model in action.

After several years in the classroom at New Tech High, Curtis has moved on to become the director of curriculum for the New Technology Foundation, where he is helping to disseminate the model. His professional growth is not uncommon, Tipton (2006) points out. "We nurture and attract the upward-bound type of teacher," she says. "Some will go into administration, others into research or writing. Many of our current staff members are working on advanced degrees." Tipton herself is a doctoral student. "This is a model," she adds, "that seems to attract learners."

GETTING READY

What will help you make the transition to using the redefined project approach with your students? How can you assess your own readiness for making this shift?

As a first step, you need to get comfortable in the learner role as you start mapping your own journey toward project-based, technology-rich learning. You may find yourself rethinking many aspects of how you teach, including how you have employed projects in the past. You won't know all the answers in the beginning. You may encounter questions that take you in unexpected directions and open more opportunities for your own learning.

It's no accident that getting comfortable with change is a theme that recurs throughout this book. Being able to adapt to change is essential for your students' future success. It's just as important for your own professional growth.

In the chapters ahead, you will get help with every aspect of designing, implementing, and assessing projects that meet the complex needs of digital-age learners. You will learn to use the newly updated National Educational Technology Standards for Students (NETS•S) to plan projects that cultivate important 21st-century skills such as creativity, information fluency, critical thinking, and digital citizenship.

But for now, let's consider the big picture of teaching with authentic projects. Where are you apt to notice change? What do you need to be ready to think about? Using the project approach will prompt you to reconsider:

- your learning goals. Be ready to rethink your expectations for what students will know and do.

- the way you talk and engage with students. Be ready to step off the stage and interact with your students differently.

- your classroom management style. Be ready to help students become better at managing their own progress.

- the physical arrangement of your class. Be ready to reconfigure the hardware—desks, computers, and other furnishings—to facilitate teamwork and collaboration.

- how you think about assessment. Be ready to reevaluate what you need to pay attention to throughout the learning process.

- what you collect. Be ready to reconsider which artifacts of learning are worth keeping.

- how you communicate with parents and colleagues. Be ready to explain your reasoning for taking the 21st-century project approach.

So much changes with this approach that you may be wondering, is it worth all the trouble? Your colleagues, principal, students, or parents may ask you the same question.

For example, a teacher from the Philippines imagined how a collaborative, online project would increase her students' literacy skills. By connecting them with fellow learners at a distant school, she envisioned greater student engagement and motivation to write well. However, she had to overcome parents' reservations about technology to get the project off the ground. Many parents equated computer use with games and video arcades, which they saw as distractions. As the teacher, Cecilia Mag-isa Estoque, explained to a reporter, "I needed to prove to the community that technology had a good and educational side, especially when properly tapped and utilized." ("Teacher Uses," 2006)

As you design and introduce successful projects and see your students engage more deeply in meaningful learning, you will discover your own good reasons to continue on this journey. You may find that projects help your students get at ideas and make connections they would not otherwise see.

Julie Lindsay has been using the project approach for a decade while teaching at international high schools around the globe. During the 2006–07 school year, she was teaching at International School Dhaka, Bangladesh, when she collaborated with Vicki Davis, a teacher from Camilla, Georgia, in the U.S., to create the Flat Classroom Project. Pairs of students from opposite sides of the globe used podcasts and wiki entries to share their thinking about Thomas Friedman's provocative book, *The World is Flat*. Even Friedman himself responded, which was one of many surprises the project generated. The Flat Classroom Project (http://flatclassroomproject.wikispaces.com) received the 2006 Edublog Award for Best Wiki.

For Lindsay (2006), projects frequently generate unexpected benefits. She reports, "I never fail to be thrilled at the absolute delight the students get from these projects and how the learning outcomes are usually far higher than initially expected." She describes the following examples of the "extra learning" that occurs apart from the content of the project:

- Students develop good communication skills to break through cultural misunderstanding and find consensus.

- Students develop good inquiry skills, which foster a sense of wonderment at the differences in the world.

- Students learn to be flexible with their working hours because they know other people are relying on them to meet their deadlines.

- Students develop a fuller understanding of how the world works and that it does not just revolve around them.

- Students achieve the feeling that, through communication with and understanding of other people, individuals can do something about changing the world.

YOUR INVESTMENT

If you are a newcomer to the project approach, it may take some time before you see similar results. In the beginning, keep in mind that you are *investing*. Project design is front-loaded work. This means the teacher invests in preparation and planning to set the stage for a project. After that, you shift control to students. Then, it's their turn to invest effort in the learning experience, and you become more of a facilitator and guide, as well as a sounding board for their questions. Your initial investment in project design begins to pay off right away, as soon as you set the stage for student-driven learning.

You can also expect the effort you are putting in now to result in efficiencies in the future. If you create a successful project, chances are you will use it again and again. It's a cumulative process: what you learn from each project informs the next one. Creating new projects is like building your classroom library. It's a resource that gets better and better over time.

For example, four teachers on a grade-level elementary team regularly work together to plan interdisciplinary projects that address multiple content standards while also connecting students to the larger world. A perennial favorite is a project about international trade. Fourth-graders become "import detectives" to figure out where in the world familiar objects come from. They use Web resources to track shipments in real time and trade information and artifacts with students in other countries. The teachers' initial investment in planning has paid off with a reliable platform on which they can build new ideas. The project has evolved over the years as teachers have found new ways—and new technologies—to take student investigations deeper. For example, when Google Earth made satellite imagery freely accessible, it gave their students a new way to "see" international trade patterns.

With practice, engaging in project work helps teachers and students develop new ways of working together and incorporating new ideas. Over time, your students will get better at working as a team, managing deadlines, resolving conflicts, and investigating their own questions. You will become better at facilitating their success. You will all get into a rhythm of working together well.

Finally, remember that you are creating new traditions for your students. Years from now, what do you hope they will remember about the learning experiences they shared with you?

WHAT'S NEXT?

Now that you have established your readiness for this reinvented project approach, it's time to think about who will be taking this journey with you. The next chapter focuses on working with colleagues and harnessing the benefits of professional learning communities.

Technology Focus

Social Bookmarking

As you roam the Web in search of good ideas, manage what you find with the help of a bookmark management tool. And, surprise! You will meet others out there who are paying attention to the same ideas as you. Furl and del.icio.us are easy bookmarking tools, and for the super-social bookmarkers out there, there's Digg. Bookmarking tools, along with other services (such as Flickr) that

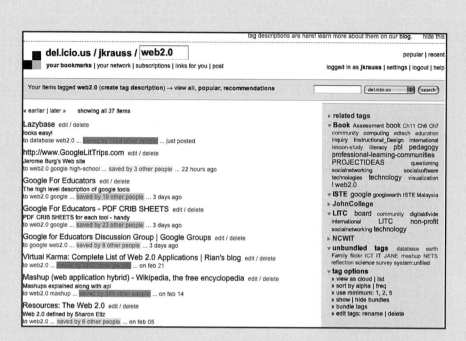

Figure 1 One page of the author's del.icio.us bookmarks, organized by the shared tag "web2.0"

allow tagging, exemplify the "folksonomy" aspect of Web 2.0. "Folksonomy" refers to the social taxonomy or classification system that evolves as users collectively make sense of what they find on the Web. Users associate "tags" or keywords to the content they bookmark, and they can see how others have treated the same material. The easiest way to understand the power of bookmarks and tagging is by using it. Try del.icio.us now and explore the social side of information on the Web.

To use del.icio.us, first create a free account and add the del.icio.us button to your browser menu bar. Then, when you find a link you like, make a digital bookmark for it by clicking the "tag" button in your browser menu bar. This will automatically save the bookmarked link to your own "my del.icio.us" page, as shown in Figure 1. You can make notes about the content and categorize links by "tagging" them with a key word or two. This makes them easy to sort through later, and your notes help you remember why you wanted them ("Refer to in Chapter 1," you might write). For example, if you find project-based learning resources you like, you might bookmark and tag them as "PBL." In your "my del.icio.us" page, you can sort those links tagged "PBL" into a single view (as opposed to the basic view where they are jumbled with your "Italian Cooking," "Spa Vacation," and other bookmarks). When others bookmark the same site as you, you will see a note next to the bookmark that says something like, "saved by 185 other people." When you sort tags, you can see your bookmarks, bookmarks made by others who used the same tag, and the most popular sites bookmarked with that tag. Tags add collective judgment to the process of deciding what's useful on the Web. If many others bookmark a site, it might be worth your attention. For example, the PBL Checklists site (http://pblchecklist.4teachers.org) was bookmarked by 85 others.

There are other social functions in tools like del.icio.us that you will discover once you start bookmarking. Start by organizing your links, and see where it leads!

> del.ici.ous—http://del.icio.us
>
> Furl—www.furl.net
>
> Digg—http://digg.com

Your Turn

Start with the Big Picture

As you begin this learning journey, spend some time thinking about where you are going. Make sure you're embarking on the right path. Do some research to gather your own evidence about the benefits of digital-age projects. Start by taking a look at these online resources to help you see the big picture of what projects have to offer you and your students:

- Education blogs (see suggestions in Side Trip, page 13). Many edu-bloggers are on the leading edge of innovative project design. Following their conversations will help you track emerging ideas and practices, and can even provide you with virtual professional development—at no cost.

- Edutopia, the George Lucas Educational Foundation Web site, offers multimedia resources that demonstrate the potential of project-based learning. Go to http://edutopia.org, then click on "Project-Based Learning." Watch a video, read a research synthesis, or browse the library of project examples. What catches your attention as a strategy that could work well with your students? What seems "too big" or out of reach at the moment?

- Project-Based Learning Online incorporates the research-based model developed by the Buck Institute for Education. Start at www.pbl-online. org. Take a look at "What do PBL Teachers Say?" (http://pbl-online. org/what_teachers_say/what_teachers_say.htm). Do you find yourself agreeing? Disagreeing? Find more research at the Buck Institute site, www.bie.org.

- National Educational Technology Standards for Students were refreshed by ISTE in 2007. Take a look at the new NETS•S (online at www.iste.org and also in appendix B in this book). We will focus on the new NETS•S in more detail in chapter 3. For now, ask yourself: How do these new standards reflect your students and the increasingly digital world in which they are living and learning?

Part of information literacy is knowing how to analyze and evaluate resources. Once you have found something you consider useful, you want to be able to locate it again. You also want to be able to share compelling research and good ideas with colleagues. Technology can help you with these activities. If you don't already have an online place to organize and annotate resources and other useful links, now's the time to set up a social bookmarking account. You will continue to use it throughout your learning journey.

CHAPTER 2

Creating a Professional Learning Community

Canadian middle school teacher Jeff Whipple came to teaching after an earlier career in engineering. Teamwork is common practice in the 21st-century workplace in engineering and many other fields, but it remains the exception in education. In his teaching career, Whipple has seen the benefits that collaboration offers teachers and, by extension, their students. At the same time, he has witnessed the challenges and changes that can get in the way of creating and sustaining professional learning communities.

Whipple's first teaching job was in a multiage classroom where he shared 60 students with two other teachers. Nothing in his formal preparation for teaching had addressed cross-grade collaboration, but he soon appreciated the benefits of working closely with colleagues. "After about a month in this classroom, it dawned on me how lucky I was," he says. "Having somebody to brainstorm with about planning, having colleagues to reflect with about what was going on in the classroom—that was great."

Two years later, Whipple was transferred to a school where he taught five periods a day of eighth-grade science in a self-contained classroom. "I nearly died! It was so isolating," he says. "It was hard to find time to share ideas or even talk to other teachers. It felt handcuffing and stagnant." The following school year, change happened again. Whipple's principal offered him a chance to team up with a colleague in a demonstration classroom that was part of a 1:1 laptop initiative. His reaction? "I jumped at the opportunity."

Currently a technology mentor for teachers in several schools participating in the laptop initiative, Whipple continues to look for ways to build collaboration into the lives of teachers. Formal opportunities for teachers to work together remain scarce. From his international conversations in the edublogging community, Whipple knows this is true in many countries. "If I could do one thing for teachers to make school better for students," Whipple says, "I'd find a way to have teachers have more time to work with each other and to develop collaborative projects."

CHANGE HAPPENS

New contexts for learning create new opportunities for teachers to work together and overcome the traditional isolation of the profession. Technology initiatives, for instance, typically include professional development along with hardware or software so that teachers can get comfortable using new tools. The HP Technology for Teaching Grants are one example. The grants are awarded to teams of five teachers who work together on project design and implementation. Professional collaboration and mentoring are part of the accompanying professional development experience. (See Spotlight: Changing Their Worldview.)

Similarly, many school restructuring efforts organize teachers and students into academies where time and opportunities for teacher collaboration are built into the regular school day. The ambitious U.S. high school reform initiative funded by the Bill & Melinda Gates Foundation is one example. A recent publication explains the reasoning behind this investment of millions of dollars into smaller, redesigned schools and academies:

> Small size facilitates collaboration, allowing faculty to share ideas about teaching and to serve as friendly critics by offering suggestions about how to improve lessons and classroom management. Teacher collaboration can also be instrumental in evaluating students' work. Through collaboration, teachers see the type and quality of work that students can produce in different settings with different teachers, a practice that almost always results in a greater appreciation of students' talents and raised expectations of even the lowest-performing students. (Bill & Melinda Gates Foundation, 2005)

Sometimes, change happens because an individual teacher takes the initiative to try something new. By incorporating digital-age projects into your curriculum, you are already planning for change. If you started on this journey because you are concerned about your students' acquisition of 21st-century skills, you understand the importance of teamwork and collaboration in their lives. The new NETS•S focus specifically on communication and collaboration as standards that students need to achieve in order to live productively in an increasingly digital world. Common sense tells you that these same skills are worth cultivating in your own practice.

Whatever your impetus for change, you will find it an advantage to work with colleagues as you explore and implement project-based learning practices. The themes, discussion guides, and activities in this book follow the arc of a project, and reading this book can be a collaborative project in itself. From the initial self-reflection to a final look back, you can use this book as a guide for trying out new learning opportunities. Read and discuss this book together with colleagues as you develop a shared vision and take steps toward common goals. By working together, you and your colleagues can expect to produce something greater than the sum of your parts.

Spotlight

Changing Their Worldview

Elise Mueller was a young teacher when she had her first experience with collaboration as a springboard for professional growth. In her second year of teaching, she received a Gates Foundation Leadership Grant. That brought her together with fellow educators from Washington State for ongoing professional development. In small group work, Mueller learned more about project-based learning and strategies for effective technology integration. "That was so wonderful," she says, "but also so rare in education." When the grant cycle ended, so did the opportunity for formal collaboration. "I was back to being in my own classroom, by myself."

The following year, Mueller happened to see an announcement about the HP Technology for Teaching Grants. The grants required team participation, and Mueller jumped at the opportunity. She approached colleagues in person at her Bellingham, Washington, elementary school to talk up the prospect. Eventually, she recruited a five-person team (one teacher from each grade from first through fourth, with fifth-grade teacher Mueller as the team lead), and they were funded for a yearlong cycle. The grant included hardware (tablet computers, projectors, and digital cameras) and professional development through ISTE. Teachers were matched with an ISTE mentor, author and educator Susan Brooks-Young. Their standards-based focus was on using technology to support science education for English language learners. Explains Mueller, "We wanted to take science vocabulary and use technology to articulate it through the grade levels. With our ELL students, we wanted to really focus on the vocabulary they need."

Right away, the teachers were immersed in their own rich learning experience. "We were given this hardware—the tablets—that we didn't know how to use. And there was no district curriculum about integrating technology into science. So we formed our own support group and learned together. That was invaluable," Mueller says. "This experience forced us to become learners. That made a huge change in how I looked at my own role in the classroom."

The team would meet informally after school. "We would bring out the tablets and just share what we were doing with our kids. It was support and learning we couldn't get anywhere else," Mueller recounts. "For me, it was a tipping point. Working together didn't cost us anything other than time, but it made a huge difference in our classrooms. This was nourishment for us. It changed my worldview."

What helped make the professional learning community so successful? Mueller cites a shared passion as one critical element. "We pushed each other to take projects to the next level. We were never comfortable with something being 'just OK,'" she says. "We share a passion for learning—we have that 'gotta know' attitude. We want to know what's out there, and what we can bring in to our classrooms to help our kids learn." What's more, the team was able to learn from what did not work well. "That failure piece is critical," Mueller explains. "If something didn't work well, you have to be able to look at what you learned and move on. This will inform your next project."

For Mueller and her colleagues, collaboration has become an ongoing part of how they approach teaching. Although she has changed schools since the grant experience, Mueller continues to connect regularly with at least two of her former team members and her ISTE mentor. In her new school setting, she is working within a model designed to foster teacher collaboration. She shares teaching responsibilities for students in Grades 3–5 with two colleagues. Mueller focuses on reading, writing, and technology; another teaches math; the third teaches science. They have regular planning time to collaborate on interdisciplinary projects.

In addition, she has developed an online community of educators with whom she connects frequently. "I connect with colleagues all over the world," she says. "Online communication has opened up a whole new world." For teachers who are new to collaboration, Mueller offers this advice: "It can be a hurdle to start connecting with other teachers. But once you find others who share your passion, you won't want to be without it."

ASSESS YOUR READINESS FOR TEAMWORK

In Chapter 1, you assessed your readiness to change how you interact with students. Now, take some time to reconsider how you interact with your colleagues as you move toward a more collaborative practice. Expect that you will scrutinize each other's instructional choices and classroom practices. Do you know how to give and receive critical feedback? Expect to plan lessons together and give and receive advice on how they go over with students. Are you comfortable with this kind of shared decision making? It doesn't have to be uncomfortable if you enter into collaboration with an open mind and respect for the colleagues who are sharing this journey with you.

For Whipple, the essential conditions that make collaboration possible come down to one word: respect. "You have to be able to be honest with one another, and that means you have to trust and appreciate the people you're working with," he says. "You need to be comfortable saying, 'That worked OK, but maybe try this next time.' It's a wonderful experience as a teacher to have that kind of feedback."

Julie Lindsay, the international educator who created the Flat Classroom Project while she was teaching in Bangladesh, found a willing collaborator halfway around the globe. It all started when Lindsay happened upon a blog entry where Vicki Davis, a teacher from the U.S., described her students' responses to reading *The World is Flat*. Lindsay explains, "I contacted her and suggested we develop a collaboration between our students so that they could interact and discuss and develop links with other students from 'the other side of the flat world.'"

The two teachers became better acquainted during the weeks of planning that led up to project launch. Lindsay says they share "the same hands-on approach, which is one of the reasons the project was such a success."

What's more, Davis emphasizes, both teachers work in contexts that emphasize rigorous academics while allowing room for innovation. Davis teaches at Westwood Schools, a private K–12 school serving about 350 students in rural Georgia. Davis herself is a graduate of the school. When she needed to find a school that could accommodate the needs of her own children—two of whom are both gifted and have special needs—she returned to her alma mater because of its long history of providing differentiated instruction. "Everything we do is research-based," she explains. The staff has taken part in hundreds of hours of professional development on topics such as cooperative learning, differentiated instruction, project-based learning, and reading strategies. In her computer science classes, Davis incorporates all those best practices. At the same time, she has a specific objective to bring in cutting-edge technologies. "About every two weeks, I teach a module on a new technology or trend."

The invitation from Bangladesh reached Georgia at "the perfect time," Davis continues. Before starting the project, she wrote a proposal for how the Flat Classroom Project would provide authentic assessment and help her students meet curriculum objectives. "I got approval from our curriculum director and headmaster first," Davis emphasizes. "I'm not a renegade teacher. I had an objective, a purpose, specific learning strategies, and so did Julie."

To bridge the geographic distance between them, they used online chat to communicate daily. "Being on the other side of the world, it would be morning for me and evening for Vicki, so we would discuss the day's work for one just as the other was about to go to work," explains Lindsay "It worked very well. Being able to solve little problems and exchange ideas on the run was an essential component of this project. We also supported each other through the project with encouragement and became good friends. This is what we tried to encourage our students to do."

With intention and trust, your team will become a successful "learning organization" that improves student achievement through the project approach.

SCHOOL AS A LEARNING ORGANIZATION

A "learning organization," or professional learning community, as it is often referred to in education, is different from other professional relationships. Peter Senge (2004) articulated a vision of the "learning organization" in business in his bestseller *The Fifth Discipline*. A learning organization can be any business work team, big or small, that engages in ongoing, collaborative problem solving focused on making the business better. In the process, individuals and the team expand their capacity to create the results they desire. They learn new patterns of thinking, they learn how to capitalize on the wisdom of the group, and, most importantly, they continually learn *how to learn together*.

The concept of learning organizations was revolutionary when it hit the business community in the 1990s. What's interesting is that it started *there* and then migrated to education. Why did it take an organizational development expert in business to imagine the promise of learning organizations in education? Isn't a school a learning organization? Think about how often you and your colleagues are able to focus on your professional practice together. How often do you have time to *learn to learn together*?

The circumstances of school—from the structure of the school day to the traction of traditional teaching practices—do not foster a collaborative examination of the fundamental acts of teaching. Teachers may spend several hours together each week, but most of their time is spent addressing scheduling and program coordination, troubleshooting individual student issues, planning school events, and tending to other matters that fall under "housekeeping." Little time is left to talk about what they are trying to teach and how they go about it. Professional learning communities change that formula.

Creating a professional learning community means making time for new ways of working with colleagues. Traditional professional development activities make up approximately 5% of a teacher's non-student contact time each year. Programs are often single-shot and mandated rather than selected by the participant, and the content often focuses on adding something new rather than improving what a teacher is already doing. Professional learning can certainly support your shift to project-based instruction, but the fundamental program changes you make will require frequent and intentional collaboration with your colleagues.

As you proceed in your exploration of project-based learning, intentionally restructure your interactions with fellow teachers. Find time to watch and reflect on each other's classroom interactions. Learn to give each other critical feedback. Capitalize on the wisdom of the group. Engage in new patterns of thinking. Learn how to continually learn together. If you work in a setting where shared time with colleagues is scarce, you may have to start small—perhaps talking with a peer about a shared instructional challenge. If you have regular times to meet with grade-level or subject-area teams, ask for feedback about a project you have in mind—and welcome feedback or participation from those who express interest. Gradually, you will reap the rewards of being a learning organization.

Some schools value collaboration so highly that they develop a process for sharing critical feedback. Carmel Crane had been teaching for a decade when she joined the faculty of a model high school in California that emphasizes teacher collaboration as part of the school culture. Early in the school year, she was getting ready to launch a digital media project with her students. Crane describes what happened next: "Before I introduced the project to students, I presented it to about 10 teachers. I laid out all the planning details, and they gave me critical feedback. It was a great opportunity to see things that I may have overlooked. They offered some ideas about how I could expand the project out to the community. And, it was a chance to make my interests public. Other teachers could see how we might work together on future projects to reach our shared goals."

The experience was eye-opening for Crane. "I'd never had that kind of peer review at any other school," she says. "It's one of the most valuable things I've experienced, in terms of developing my curriculum and really improving as a teacher. It's the best professional experience I've ever had."

COMMUNITIES WITHIN COMMUNITIES

You already belong to more than one community of practice. Minimally, all teachers are part of a faculty that works together on a day-to-day basis as they march through the school year. A fifth-grade teacher forms another, more close-knit community of practice with her grade-level teaching peers at her school. A ninth-grade biology teacher may feel affinity with other science teachers in the district and participate in an even larger community of practice with science teachers across the country. A teacher interested in blogging may find her community of practice online among educators far away.

Belonging to a community of practice can make your professional life more productive and satisfying. But to really reap the benefits of partnerships, don't stop there. Professional learning communities focus on three big, student-centered ideas: ensure that students learn, create a culture of collaboration for school improvement, and focus on results (DuFour, 2004). What sets these communities apart from more casual communities of practice is the shift from looking at what you teach to focusing on what your students learn. Consider taking the next step and joining a more tightly focused professional learning community that comes together to focus on 21st-century projects.

A project-based learning collaboration among students is a lot like a professional learning community among teachers. For both, the learning is relevant and rigorous, and the "students" learn to learn together. Both groups develop the skills and dispositions necessary in the "real world," including communication, problem solving, project management, motivation, and persistence. Both build bonds as they share triumphs and disappointments. (For an example, see Spotlight 1: Changing Their Worldview in this chapter.)

Project-based learning puts new demands on teachers, students, and the schools themselves. A single teacher cannot realize the full potential of this approach in the isolation of his or her classroom. Efforts are hampered by the limitations of the classroom space, and it can be frustrating to fit a "square peg" program into the school's "round hole" of schedule, spaces, and resources.

By enlisting like-minded colleagues to lobby together for necessary changes, you create a critical mass of dedicated educators who share a common goal. This has practical benefits as well as more philosophical ones. Making changes in schedules and use of space and resources is easier if a block of classrooms, teachers, and students are in agreement. A group of teachers can catalyze wider change, spreading good ideas further than a single teacher can. A project-based learning program delivered by a high-functioning professional learning community of teachers can be the "engine of improvement" (DuFour & Eaker, 1998) that drives a school forward.

Among professional learning communities that function for several years, benefits include the following:

- decreased teacher isolation

- increased commitment to the mission

- shared responsibility

- more powerful learning

- a higher likelihood of fundamental, systemic change

  (Hord, 1997)

Technology Focus

Online Communities

Online tools allow you to set up or join an existing space to support your professional learning community. Participating in these online communities will connect you to a wider network of colleagues who share your professional interests. These spaces are emerging examples of peer-to-peer professional development. They show how teachers as active learners don't wait for professional development to come to them; instead, teachers create their own opportunities for shared learning. What's more, you will gain experience with the social networking tools that many of your students are already using to create and communicate with their own online communities.

Classroom 2.0 (http://classroom20.ning.com) and the Global Education Collaborative (http://globaleducation.ning.com) are two of many social networking sites that have been designed by educators, for educators. Both use an online service called Ning, which allows users to create groups, identify "friends," and start and respond to discussions, among other features. Classroom 2.0 focuses on practical applications of computer technology (especially Web 2.0), both in the classroom and in teachers' own professional development. The Global Educational Collaborative fosters conversation and collaboration around global awareness in teaching and learning.

Tapped In is an online professional development space developed by SRI International's Center for Technology in Learning (http://tappedin.org/tappedin). K–12 teachers, librarians, administrators, and professional development staff, as well as university faculty, students, and researchers, gather here to learn, collaborate, share, and support one another.

Using Tapped In, educators use electronic tools for communication and collaboration techniques such as threaded discussion, file sharing, sharing of Web pages, and synchronous chats, all with a focus on effective teaching and learning. In addition, participating organizations use Tapped In to deliver online professional development courses or provide online mentoring.

HOW TO START?

Professional learning communities range from formal to informal. A school reform effort may include a formal protocol, such as a critical friends approach to teacher feedback. Or, two colleagues may decide to meet weekly for coffee and conversation about 21st-century projects. Some professional learning communities exist in cyberspace, where like-minded educators come together to exchange ideas and encourage each other toward excellence.

Anne Davis, an advocate of blogging with elementary students, suggests using your own blog as a tool for making connections with like-minded colleagues. That's how she first connected with Will Richardson, another early member of the edublogging community. Although the two teachers had not yet met in person, and although their schools were separated by hundreds of miles, they collaborated to develop a successful project in which high school journalism students mentored elementary writers. "If you are a blogger yourself, you will develop a network with other educators online," Davis says.

Your current situation and purpose will determine the composition of your group and the ways you interact. A team of two is better than no team at all, but imagine the compounding effect of a large team, an entire faculty, or an international community of colleagues.

If your "dream team" is not obvious, look first to the systems and groups that are already in place. Is the faculty formally addressing student achievement? Consider an adjunct group that offers to try a 21st-century project approach to address achievement issues that everyone shares. Do teachers meet regularly in grade-level teams or departments? Are there any interdisciplinary teams? These groups may be ready to take on project-based learning with you.

Maybe your ideal collaborators are geographically distributed, working in different schools or even in different regions of the country. This book will address ways to use technology to guide teamwork, whether it's virtual or face-to-face.

Members of your community for addressing digital-age projects should share these research-based components:

- have a clear sense of mission
- share a vision of the conditions they must create to achieve the mission
- work together in collaborative teams to determine the best practice to achieve the mission
- organize into groups headed by teacher-leaders
- focus on student learning
- are goal- and results-oriented
- collaborate with each other
- hold shared values and beliefs
- commit themselves to continuous improvement
- see themselves as life-long learners

    (DuFour, DuFour, & Eaker 2002)

Spotlight

Mashup of a Good Idea and the Right Tool

Jerome Burg, a teacher at Granada High School in California, wanted to immerse his students in *Candide, The Grapes of Wrath, Night*, and other "road" literature, so he created Google Lit Trips. Using Google Earth and embellished

Figure 2 Google Lit Trips invites others to contribute literature lessons that use Google Earth. © Jerome Burg, Google Lit Trips. Reprinted with permission.

placemarks that mark a story's "road," Google Lit Trips offers learners amazing virtual worlds to explore as they study great literature. It's a mashup of a good idea and the right tool.

To help students appreciate the devastating conditions that drove the Joads west in *The Grapes of Wrath*, Burg links newsreel footage from a 1930s dust storm to a Google Earth placemark at Bethany, Oklahoma, the starting point of the story. His placemarks link to period music, vocabulary definitions, and more to help the learning stick. Burg created an elegant Web site in order to share his "lit trips" with fellow teachers. (See Google Lit Trips at http://googlelittrips.com)

Initially, Burg thought a few teachers would find the site and submit their own "trips." Then technology maven Will Richardson highlighted Google Lit Trips in a presentation, and visits to Burg's Web site skyrocketed. A new community of practice began to take shape. "At first I imagined a few people would want to contribute, but then I realized it was taking off, with more than 3,000 Web visits in less than a week," Burg says. In less than three months, the site drew more than 20,000 visitors.

Burg realized that interest in a brand-new professional practice was emerging, and he knew he would have to figure out how to support it. He added Lit Trip Tips to the Web site and began gathering promising practices to share with others. He invited his growing audience to share their integration strategies, assessment structures, pedagogical support, ideas and strategies for having students develop their own Lit Trips, and other resources. Burg envisions the most inspired teachers joining him in building criteria and processes for developing excellent Lit Trips that exemplify best practices in teaching literature. His vision is to make the site "a community of Lit Trippin' teachers." See figure 2 for a screen shot from Google Lit Trips.

GET YOUR FEET WET

Before you launch an extended learning project that you design, you might want to start with a project that lets you practice collaboration with colleagues. You can jump-start the process by joining a well-designed project that is already underway. This reduces your investment in planning time and connects you with a community of educators who share your learning goals. You can exchange ideas with others and practice giving and receiving critical feedback. This built-in support will scaffold your learning before you build your own project plan from the ground up. Following are some examples of project sources from around the world. Many projects include opportunities for online collaboration, along with supporting materials for teachers.

- Center for Innovation in Engineering and Science Education (CIESE, www. k12science.org)—CIESE hosts projects in which students around the world contribute local data and analyze amassed world data with other student researchers around the globe. A few project titles include The International Boiling Point Project, The Square of Life, The Human Genetics Project, and The Noonday Project.

- Flat Stanley (http://flatstanley.enoreo.on.ca)—This global literacy project connects students and schools in dozens of countries on several continents. The Flat Stanley Web site includes a forum for exchanging project ideas with colleagues worldwide, and the site is available in English and French. Search the tag "flatstanley" on the Flickr photo sharing site (www.flickr.com) and explore the worldwide adventures of hundreds of traveling Stanleys.

- Global Learning and Observations to Benefit the Environment (GLOBE, www. globe.gov)—This organization promotes hands-on science education worldwide. Primary and secondary students engage in projects that involve taking scientifically valid measurements in fields such as atmosphere, hydrology, soils, and land cover. Students report their data online and collaborate with scientists and other GLOBE students around the world. Resources for teachers include videos and other professional development, along with support from working scientists and mentor teachers. The resources are available in six languages.

- Global SchoolNet (www.globalschoolnet.org/gsh/pr/)—The Internet Project Registry at Global SchoolNet is a clearinghouse for collaborative projects from around the globe. Teachers who want to collaborate online can join an existing project, take a look at upcoming projects, or review more than 2,000 archives of completed projects. New project management tools will be introduced soon, with funding from Microsoft Partners in Learning. Global SchoolNet has reached more than one million students from 45,000 schools in 194 countries.

- Intercultural E-mail Classroom Connections (IECC, www.iecc.org)—Since 1992, the IECC service has helped teachers around the globe arrange intercultural e-mail connections among their students. A new service, IECC-INTERGEN, helps teachers and their classrooms create intergenerational partnerships with volunteers who are over 50 years of age.

- International Education and Research Network (iEARN, www.iearn.org)— Collaborative online projects involve thousands of students on several continents. Professional development resources, both online and off, are available for teachers. Teacher-developed projects focus on developing students' language, literacy, research, and critical-thinking skills; providing students opportunities to use new technologies; and building students' cultural awareness and community awareness. Resources are available in many languages. The names of the following recent collaborative projects will inspire your thinking: Back Talk Journal: The International News Magazine; Celebrations and Mourning; Cities Near the Sea; Comfort Quilt Project; Feeding Minds, Fighting Hunger; Migrating Birds Know No Boundaries; Talking Kites Around the World; and The Time Machine Project.

- Journey North (www.learner.org/jnorth/)—Collaborative projects for K–12 focus on aspects of seasonal change, such as tracking the migration of Monarch butterflies in real time. Multi-media resources include photos, videos, animations, and interactive learning features. Many projects ask students to add data, putting them in the roles of researchers. Materials for teachers include background lessons on core concepts and suggestions for developing students' observation skills through questioning.

- Oz Projects (www.ozprojects.edna.edu.au/sibling/home)—This Australian site helps educators from around the world find or post online collaborative projects.

- Web-based Inquiry Science Environment (WISE, http://wise.berkeley.edu/welcome.php)—Students in Grades 5–12 participate in projects that involve analyzing scientific controversies and examining real-world evidence. Simulations and modules engage students in collaborative inquiry.

Your Turn

Reading Group

Read and discuss this book in a reading group. You may already be engaging in collaborative planning with colleagues, and book study becomes a guided exercise. Or, you may be coming together initially to read and discuss this book, and you later decide to continue working together to plan and implement a project. In either situation, use your shared reading group experience as a foundation for reflecting with colleagues on your professional practice. As you discuss new ideas, try to keep your focus on student learning. Appendix C suggests chapter-by-chapter questions to help guide your conversations.

Section II

Packing Up

As you begin planning a pilot project, Section II helps you define the conceptual framework and guides you through the design process. Before you introduce the project to your students, invest time to consider the project management skills, strategies, and technologies that will lead you and your students to success.

CHAPTER 3

Imagining the Possibilities

How do you prepare for a trip? As you pack, you probably imagine the destination and your means of traveling there. You think about the conditions you expect to find. Before "packing up" for your project with concrete planning, picture your destination—the learning ahead—and consider different ways of getting there with your students. With a clear mental image, you'll be ready to decide just what you need to take along.

This chapter focuses on establishing the conceptual framework of a project. At the end of chapter 3, you will follow a set of prompts that help you identify the central concepts your project will address. In the next chapter, you will dig into planning.

WHAT IS MOST IMPORTANT?

Good projects get to the heart of a discipline. The more complex and important an idea, the better suited it is for the 21st-century project treatment. Identifying the big ideas—the core concepts and processes—at the heart of the subjects we teach is the first step of project planning.

Think for a moment: What big ideas, what core concepts and processes, should students know after studying with you? If your students understood or could do just two or three things, what would those be? In Earth science, for example, a core concept is energy in the Earth system. Important processes include designing an investigation and using instruments as scientists do. An algebra teacher might say applying linear equations is important. An elementary teacher wants students to increase their reading and writing fluency as they develop literacy skills. A history teacher expects students to appreciate how history shapes culture and to understand the techniques of historians.

When you teach from published curriculum, judgments about what is important have been made for you. This can be an efficient system, but students learn no more than what the textbook publisher imagined for them. The results are predictable and, often, generic. Published curriculum and content standards dive straightaway into a sequence of learning objectives. In textbooks, the material is broken into digestible bits. Synthesis for understanding important, overarching "big ideas" is left to the masterful teacher and very insightful learner.

Projects, on the other hand, are highly contextual. They are created through a series of decisions. Projects are designed for students by their teachers, the people who best understand their learning needs. Good projects connect directly to the students' frames of reference, interests, and experiences. Teachers who use the project approach might also use textbooks. But instead of being the foundation of a course, the textbook becomes a reference book rich with illustrations and supplying information written at the reading and conceptual level of students.

WHAT'S THE "BIG IDEA"?

Thinking about the "big ideas" of your curriculum is a good workout. Scan the tables of contents of your teaching guides. Review the curriculum standards for your subjects. Ask your colleagues: *What do these add up to?*

Kathy Cassidy, an early elementary teacher from Saskatchewan, Canada, wanted her second-graders to get the "big idea" of what the number 1,000 means. How could she make this number more concrete for her young learners? "We don't have a lot of space in the classroom to collect things, so I thought of collecting names on a wiki," she explains. The result was a simple wiki page called, appropriately, 1,000 Names. She started by showing students how to use the edit feature to add their own names—one to a box on the page. Then, she invited parents to join the project, too. Next, she invited three more classrooms at her school to add their names to the page. As word spread online, she says, "It exploded from there." Grandparents, friends, and others joined in from several countries. Once every week, Cassidy would show her students the wiki (using her projector), which allowed her repeat opportunities to reinforce the meaning of 1,000. They watched as the number of names grew—starting with fewer than 100 and reaching more than 850 within three months. As the number of names approached the goal of 1,000, student interest swelled, too.

Technology Focus

Why Use a Wiki?

A wiki is a Web resource that allows users to add and edit content collectively and online, from any computer with an Internet connection. It is useful for planning a project, whether you work alone or collaborate locally or at a distance. The ease of use and accessibility of a wiki makes it a helpful tool for organizing your thinking and tracking your actions. See chapter 5 for more about wikis. For an in-depth guide to creating a wiki, read Will Richardson's *Blogs, Wikis, Podcasts, and Other Powerful Web Tools for Classrooms* (Corwin Press, 2006). When you're ready to set up your own space, PBWiki (http://pbwiki.com) offers free accounts, as well as resources for educators. Or, try your hand with user-friendly Wikispaces (www.wikispaces.com).

Every grade level and subject area focuses on big ideas, and so do disciplines in the world outside school. After you identify the overarching concepts and processes you want your students to understand, reflect on why these concepts are important. This will get you thinking about their application or relevance in real life and help you imagine engaging and realistic ways students might grapple with the topics. It will help you to reveal the interdisciplinary aspects of the topic, too. Think: *Who cares about this? Who does it touch?*

Robert Griffin, who teaches in the fishing community of Grand Manan Island in Canada, uses authentic projects as often as he can. "As an everyday assignment such as letter writing, I have my students relate to authentic purpose by writing a letter to the Minister of Fisheries on a license issue or a quota issue. These are issues my students would often hear discussed at the supper table," he explains. Griffin's main criterion for determining whether projects are authentic is "whether the activities take place in the real world. As an example, do journalists submit articles to the newspaper to be published? Yes, and thereby so do my students." If the editor of the county newspaper chooses to publish an article, he says, "the student receives a $15 stipend from the newspaper as well as a grade from me for their course. Seeing their articles in the newspaper is authentic assessment. The publication of the article says that their article was good enough to be published."

Think again about the big Earth science idea: energy in the Earth system. Who outside of school pays attention to this fundamental idea? In Earth science, a seismologist may pay attention to energy as it relates to plate tectonics and tsunamis. People who live along shorelines care about tsunamis, too. So do community zoning boards, emergency response agencies, insurance companies, and the fishing and hospitality industries. Imagine how a "hands-on, minds-on" project might evolve to take diverse interests such as these into account.

Thinking about real-world contexts helps to reveal the interdisciplinary nature of a project. Unlike traditional learning, in which ideas are sorted into "pure" disciplines, project learning, like real life, gets messy and overlaps multiple disciplines. It's in this overlapping space that great projects are born.

In physical science education, learning about energy might be an end in itself. But imagine introducing elementary students to energy in the context of designing simple stoves that rely on the sun for heat. Now imagine incorporating environmental science as students learn about the effects of burning wood for fuel. Get students thinking about where in the world people rely on wood for cooking, and you have integrated geography. Take it a step further with technology, and now students are hosting a videoconference to share their stove designs with peers on another continent, incorporating language arts and multimedia skills. Now you have set in motion a rich project with a real purpose, which is exactly what happened when a Florida elementary school became involved in an international solar cooking project. (To see project archives, visit the Miami Country Day School Web site: http://aces.miamicountryday.org/SolarCookers/solar_cookers.htm.)

When students know that their project offers value for their community, they become even more invested in learning. For example, students are routinely asked to help solve local environmental issues at a high school with a tradition of doing community-based projects. Their projects typically incorporate science, math modeling, language arts, and civics. Students use technology to create three-dimensional maps, documentary videos, and multimedia presentations that help them advocate for their proposed solution to the local governing body.

Imagine all the learning opportunities that could unfold for your students. Don't worry if your project ideas veer into unfamiliar territory or require you to learn new skills or master unfamiliar content. This is your opportunity to collaborate with colleagues and engage experts—just as you will be asking your students to do. Once a well-designed project is underway, you become part of the learning community.

Brainstorming with colleagues will help you further expand your thinking about the learning opportunities that projects present. For example, if you are a middle or high school teacher, consider meeting with someone who teaches a different subject. Together, imagine a project that will address a goal from each of your subjects. If it doesn't work, swap out one goal and try again. Look for natural connections.

If you teach at the elementary level, meet with any other teacher. Pick any three subjects you both teach—for example, health, reading, and math; or science, art, and music. From any of these subjects, identify a topic or topics you would like to teach through projects. Now, brainstorm how you could incorporate concepts from the other subjects. What would it look like? Help one another imagine the possibilities.

PLANNING FOR RIGOR AND 21ST-CENTURY SKILLS

Just as you have considered the big ideas of the subjects you want students to understand, you also need to imagine how the project will help them develop 21st-century skills. Think beyond subject mastery to the important skills, attitudes, and habits of mind your project might involve.

A well-designed project causes students to stretch their intellectual muscles in ways traditional learning activities may not. One way to ensure rigor in a project is to plan for learning actions associated with the higher-order categories of Bloom's Taxonomy of Educational Objectives. (Note: The Taxonomy was revised in 2001 by Anderson and Krathwohl, with changes that included renaming and reordering the categories. The revised version is referenced here, with original category names in parentheses.)

The Bloom categories of objectives, moving from lower-order (more typical instructional fare) to higher order (the realm of projects) are: *Remember* (Knowledge), *Understand* (Comprehension), *Apply, Analyze, Evaluate,* and *Create* (Synthesis). Although all have their place, the last three are particularly relevant to project-based learning. Imagine how your project plan can evolve using the following higher-order thinking skills and the actions associated with them:

- **Analyze**—examine, explain, investigate, characterize, classify, compare, deduce, differentiate, discriminate, illustrate, prioritize

- **Evaluate**—judge, select, decide, justify, verify, improve, defend, debate, convince, recommend, assess

- **Create**—adapt, anticipate, combine, compose, invent, design, imagine, propose, theorize, formulate

These verbs will come in handy as you design questions that drive student actions. Imagine transforming a typical project—writing a biography of a notable person—by asking students to not just report on their research, but synthesize and evaluate.

- **Traditional biography assignment:** Study a distinguished person from the Renaissance period and write a report describing his or her life and notable achievements.

- **Reconsidered biography assignment:** Study two or three figures from the Renaissance who distinguished themselves in the same field. **Develop criteria** for "hall of fame" status, **compare** these figures' accomplishments, then **select** one individual for inclusion in a "Renaissance Hall of Fame." **Justify** your selection. **Design** an appropriate seal for the award he or she will be granted.

21ST-CENTURY LITERACIES—A SYNTHESIS

With deliberate attention, projects can truly prepare learners for the world beyond school. Any time you ask students to collaborate and create, it is likely you are touching on 21st-century skills. Begin imagining the 21st-century skills your project can address. What do the terms "21st-century skills" and "21st-century literacy" mean for today's learners?

Several research projects have generated various definitions of 21st-century skills and literacies, but all definitions go well beyond the ability to read and write. Many instructional standards, from the NETS•S to those of the American School Library Association (ASLA), are changing to focus more on the behaviors required of accomplished people in the 21st century.

The enGauge 21st-Century Skills were formulated by a team that examined research, conducted literature reviews, explored workforce trends, and interviewed educators and other constituent groups. The result is a model that highlights Digital-Age Literacy (scientific, economic, and technological literacies; visual and information literacies; and multicultural literacy and global awareness), Inventive Thinking (managing complexity; self-direction; curiosity, creativity, and risk taking; and higher-order thinking), Effective Communication (teaming, collaboration, and interpersonal skills; personal, social, and civic responsibility; and interactive communication), and High Productivity (prioritizing, planning, and managing for results; effective use of real-world tools; and ability to produce relevant, high-quality products) (North Central Regional Educational Laboratory, 2003).

The Partnership for 21st-Century Skills, an advocacy organization representing business leaders, educators, and policymakers, has developed its own Framework for 21st-Century Learning (www.21stcenturyskills.org). The framework incorporates Core Subjects (language arts, math, science, and so forth), along with 21st-Century Content (global awareness, entrepreneurial and civic literacy, and health awareness), Learning and Thinking Skills (critical thinking, problem solving, communication, creativity, collaboration, and information and media literacy), Information and Communications Technology (ICT) Literacy (effective use of technology for teaching and learning), and Life Skills (leadership, self-direction, accountability, and adaptability).

Working from a global perspective, the United Nations Educational, Scientific, and Cultural Organization (UNESCO) offers this broader definition of literacy:

> Literacy is the ability to identify, understand, interpret, create, communicate, and compute, using printed and written materials associated with varying contexts. Literacy involves a continuum of learning to enable an individual to achieve his or her goals, to develop his or her knowledge and potential, and to participate fully in the wider society. (UNESCO Literacy Assessment and Monitoring Programme [LAMP], 2004)

The ISTE NETS•S address digital literacies, as well. Released in 2007 after a year-long review process, the new NETS•S represent the most recent international thinking about the wide range of skills required to learn and live in an increasingly digital world. The standards emphasize performance and behaviors that reflect the emerging learning opportunities afforded by technology, as well as the world students will work and live in as adults. Skills such as creativity and innovation are introduced in this revision, underscoring the global need for adaptable thinkers who can address the still-unknown challenges of the 21st century.

Specifically, the NETS•S address Creativity and Innovation (creative thinking, constructing knowledge, and developing innovative processes and products), Communication and Collaboration (using digital media and environments to support individual learning and the learning of others), Research and Information Fluency (applying digital tools to gather, evaluate, and use information), Digital Citizenship (understanding human issues relating to technology and practicing ethical behavior), and Technology Operations and Concepts (understanding technology concepts, systems, and operations). (See appendix B: ISTE National Educational Technology Standards for Students.)

By these multiple definitions, *literacy* boils down to learning to be independent, aware, and productive citizens. A true-to-life project naturally involves opportunities for learners to become literate in the 21st-century sense of the word—and for teachers to accomplish their own 21st-century instructional goals.

Canadian teacher Jeff Whipple had his own epiphany about literacy after hearing author David Warlick give a conference presentation. Whipple relates: "I suddenly realized: It's all about information. We want our students to be *information artists*. Can they find information, assess whether it's good or bad, deal with raw data, and then put out their own understanding of it? As teachers, can we give students opportunities to get their own information, develop their own stories, and share their stories with others? Those are the basic literacy skills that are critical, regardless of subject matter."

Developing these capabilities in students calls on new instructional tasks for the teacher. Imagine how you might teach students to find, evaluate, and synthesize information from multiple sources. Imagine developing a project outline and rubrics that guide students and focus their attention on critical and valid information. Discuss your plans with specialists at your school, such as librarians or information specialists, and seek their advice. They will welcome the opportunity to put their expertise to work in the context of your class projects.

Your decisions about instruction and the learning tools you use are not made lightly. When you choose new technology tools or ones students or parents typically associate with other purposes, it is important to communicate about the power of using the tools to meet your instructional aims, as well as your attention to safety. As you select, be ready to say: "We are using tool X, and there is no better tool to help us meet these important outcomes." See Spotlight: Romeo in MySpace, to see how one teacher introduced a social networking tool to achieve an instructional purpose.

Spotlight

Romeo in MySpace

Koty Zelinka, an English teacher at Portland Lutheran High School in Oregon, used MySpace to help her students move deeper into analyzing Shakespearean characters. The social networking site was an obvious choice because nearly 90% of her students already had their own pages. She had them work in small teams to create pages for Romeo, Juliet, Mercutio, Tybalt, and other characters. Before long, students were channeling their Shakespearean counterparts via emoticons, photos, and star-crossed blog entries.

Using MySpace for learning not only got her students engaged in character studies, but also gave Zelinka a chance to educate students—and parents—about online security. Anticipating parents' concern, Zelinka made clear her educational rationale for using MySpace for the unit of study, and also described parameters for use (Samuels, 2007). Using MySpace in school was an opportunity to teach students about Internet security, ensuring safe use during Shakespeare studies, but also outside of school, where students are more likely to spend time online without guidance.

When choosing technology tools that support your learning aims, be sure, as Zelinka did, to plan how you will communicate the educational purpose for using them and how you will teach appropriate—and safe—use.

Authentic projects involve digital resources. According to the American Library Association, "To be information literate, a person must be able to recognize when information is needed and have the ability to locate, evaluate, and use effectively the needed information" (American Library Association, 1989).

To learn more about information literacy, review the ISTE National Education Technology Standards for Students as well as Web sites hosted by library media and information organizations (such as the American Library Association). In chapter 6, we will review the "Big6," an information literacy problem-solving strategy that helps students focus their attention on the information that serves them best. Later, when you move into more concrete project planning, you will come back to information literacy as a specific focus.

For now, ask yourself: *In what ways can a project help students learn how the world works and how they will work in the world? How can it set them up to practice skills that will make them effective, lifelong learners?*

LEARNING DISPOSITIONS

Learning encompasses understanding (your subject-matter objectives), skills (fundamentals such as reading and writing and "new" 21st-century literacies), and learning dispositions. Learning dispositions are important traits, attitudes, habits, and feelings we encourage but usually cannot teach directly, such as confidence, curiosity, resourcefulness, cooperation, motivation, persistence, and courage. Learners acquire learning dispositions less through direct teaching and more through experiences and encouragement. When you plan your project, think about learning dispositions you can cultivate in your students. As the project commences, talk about these directly with your students. When students begin to understand how they learn and can reflect on their own processes (metacognition), they become more sophisticated learners, ready for life ahead.

Spotlight

Thinking Aloud about Learning Dispositions

Guy Claxton, professor of the Learning Sciences at the University of Bristol Graduate School of Education in the UK, is the author of *Wise Up: Learning to Live the Learning Life*. In an article for the *Times Educational Supplement*, he shares this story told by Sophie, an eight-year-old who is thinking about her own "learning power":

> Six months ago, I was quite a good Team Learner, but my Stickability was pretty weak. I didn't use my Imagination much, except when I was told to, and I never Planned what resources I might need before I started in on a piece of learning. Now my Planning and Imagining are much stronger—but I still tend to drift off when I don't immediately know how to tackle something. I think I'll make Stickability my learning power target for the next half-term.
> (as cited in Claxton, 2003)

KEEP YOUR STUDENTS IN MIND

Finally, imagine the emerging project idea from your students' point of view: Why should they care? John Seely Brown, former chief scientist at Palo Alto Research Center in California, suggests that we should imagine what "passion-based learning" would look like (LaMonica, 2006). Replace the term *project* with *passion* and think about your idea again. What would spark your students' curiosity and make them feel that what they are learning is interesting and important? How would interactions with classmates and others engage them and make them feel a part of something big? What activities, experiences, and tools would excite them? When you tap your students' enthusiasm, you increase the likelihood that they will dive into deep inquiry and come away with essential understanding. Projects with passion help connect with the social and emotional sides of the learning experience.

Technology Focus

Essential Learning with Digital Tools, the Internet, and Web 2.0

It helps to examine technological tools by way of the essential learning they help students accomplish. With the information universe rapidly expanding and Web-based applications multiplying almost too quickly to track, any summary of information or tools today would be obsolete tomorrow—or rather, in five minutes. Instead of compiling an exhaustive list of tools, consider the essential learning functions technology can deliver for project-based learning. Unlike the tools themselves, essential learning functions are fairly stable. In project-based learning, having the functional ability to make things visible and discussable or to foster collaboration will always be important, even as the tools change. Once you identify a function you need, read through an assortment of tool ideas to deliver those that serve those functions best for your context. Once you identify a function you need, you can find an assortment of tools to choose from (with more arriving tomorrow) that perform the function and suit your context.

Following is a brief description of each essential learning function, how it relates to 21st-century learning, and an example of tools that deliver that function. The list is not exhaustive, but it provides a glimpse of the kinds of things you might keep in mind when making your own selections.

Appendix A presents an expanded look at the following learning functions and more details about the tools that deliver them.

ESSENTIAL LEARNING FUNCTIONS

1. Ubiquity: Learning Inside and Outside the Classroom, and All the Time

Imagine giving students the opportunity to learn anytime and anywhere. While "ubiquity" is not a learning function per se, it is an overarching and desirable quality of tools that support project learning. From handheld devices to Web-based applications, look for tools that help students be more mobile and learn wherever they are, whenever they want, and more frequently, with whomever they want.

Examples of tools that promote ubiquity include personal digital assistants, mobile phones, MP3 players, global positioning devices, and robust Web-based applications (Web mail, Google Docs, Flickr photos, and virtual "desktops" such as NetVibes).

2. Deep Learning

Most Web sites students will find explain, report, or in the case of blogs, opine. Go beyond "filtered" information (where the meaning is made by others) and help students find and make sense of "raw" information on the Web. Primary sources (e.g., digitized versions of historical documents) and rich databases (e.g., real-time seismic data) are becoming more accessible all the time. Higher-order thinking is engaged when students have to navigate and sort, organize, analyze, and make graphical representations in order to learn and express learning. As information piles higher and higher, tools have emerged to help students grapple with what they find. Examples of information students might use include educational video-on-demand, primary source archives, and real-time data sets. Examples of tools for organizing data include Web-based spreadsheet and database applications and online graphing applets.

3. Making Things Visible and Discussable

There are many good reasons to make things visible with digital tools: showing rather than telling, conceptualizing with "mind" maps, seeing things too big or too small or too fast or too slow for the naked eye, examining history through digital artifacts, expressing ideas through photography and multimedia, graphical representation and modeling, animation and digital art. A picture is worth a thousand words, and making thoughts and ideas visible and sharable is the first step in getting the conversation going. Examples of visual representation tools include Visual Thesaurus, Google Earth, Flickr, and FreeMind Mindmapper.

4. Expressing Ourselves, Sharing Ideas, Building Community

The World Wide Web has evolved from an information medium into a social medium. Opportunities for expression have never been greater. Students using MySpace and instant messaging are accustomed to these forms of personal interaction. Imagine the parallels in school, and find ways students can use the Web to express their ideas and build society around shared interests. Examples of tools that allow sharing of ideas and social interaction include blogs, social software, tagging, and virtual meetings with Webinars.

5. Collaboration—Teaching and Learning with Others

Projects invite collaboration. Tools abound that help us learn together. Plan and write together using shared applications. Use exchange services to find experts or fellow learners. Plan virtual experiences that let people "meet." Use survey tools to take the pulse of the community.

Examples of collaborative tools include wikis, Web-based "office" applications, Webinars, survey tools, expert and learning exchanges, and computer phone calls with voice-over IP.

6. Research

21st-century projects invariably involve research, and for most research questions students turn directly to the Web. Internet research puts information literacy to the test. (Students studying the cultural significance of myth? A Google Search query of the term "myth" turns up nearly 49,400,000 results!) Quality directories, search engines with filtering, a variety of bookmark tagging tools, and citation "engines" help students make sense of and organize what they need from the ever-expanding Web. Examples of research tools include ASK for Kids, del.icio.us bookmarking, and Citation Machine.

7. Project Management: Planning and Organization

Project management is a major category that gets its own treatment in chapter 5. In brief, project management helps students manage time, work, sources, feedback from others, drafts, and products during projects. A simple folder on the district server or a workspace in the school's learning management system may suffice, but consider Web-based "home pages" or "desktops" that give students a space to work and associated tools (calendars, to-do lists) to help them plan and organize. They can get to their "home page" from anywhere at any time. Examples of learning management systems include Desire2Learn and

Moodle; examples of Web-based "home pages" include Netvibes, iGoogle, My Yahoo!, and Protopage.

8. Reflection and Iteration

Deep learning happens when you examine your ideas from all sides and from other points of view. And reconsidering and reshaping ideas to bring them to high polish is the difference between acceptable and masterful work. A blog can serve as a personal diary or journal, where students put their thinking out on the table to give it a good look and elicit alternative perspectives. Blog entries spanning the life of a project can be lasting artifacts of the process. Looking back at your own thinking is worthwhile, and it has never been easier than with blogs. Wikis are useful for drafting iterations of work and sharing works in progress. Using version histories, a writer can look back at (and even retrieve) earlier drafts. Any number of people can collaborate on a wiki. Imagine the possibilities for sharing, writing, and editing together using a wiki. Examples of blog hosting sites include Edublogs, Blogger, and Blogmeister. Examples of wiki hosting sites include Wikispaces and PBwiki.

Your Turn

Start Your Plan on a Wiki

Now that you are imagining the possibilities, you are ready to plan a specific project. In the following activity, respond to prompts that revisit the major themes and narrow your focus. Planning is an iterative process. Be ready to revisit the conceptual framework of your project from time to time and even reconsider the fundamental choices you have made.

Now, as you prepare to plan a project, create your own wiki space (to use on your own or share with a team of colleagues). Use a free wiki host such as Wikispaces or PBwiki (these will let you upload a few files, which is handy). Make a simple front page and create a page for each team member. You might also want a page for each meeting you hold.

For this chapter, build a wiki page with this title: "Core Concepts to Teach This Year."

The following prompts will help you define the conceptual framework of your project. Once you have completed them, use your wiki to list the essential concepts students should know as a result of being in your class.

For individuals: Reflect on this series of questions and record your responses on your own wiki page. Be ready to share at your next team meeting. Don't become too wedded to your ideas yet.

For a group: When you meet, share and discuss your individual responses, then respond to the questions again together. If you aim for a collaborative project, try to "mash up" your efforts into one shared project idea.

1. What important and enduring concepts are fundamental to each subject you teach? List them. Try to limit the list to two to three big concepts for each subject. Refer to content standards you teach to determine those covered by these big "umbrella" concepts.

2. Why do these concepts matter? Why are they important?

3. Outside school, who cares about these topics? What is their relevance in different people's lives and in different parts of the world?

4. Select one or two of the most promising of these topics and think about real-life contexts to answer the following: What are the interdisciplinary connections? What other subjects might be incorporated?

5. As you begin to imagine working with these topics, how might you push past rote learning into analysis, evaluation, and creation? Incorporate Bloom's "rigor" verbs into your answer.

6. Imagine authentic ways students might engage in the project and the ways 21st-century skills might be addressed. Hint: The terms *collaboration, digital tools*, and *information literacy* should appear in your answer!

7. What aspects of these topics will interest your students? (A feature that seems superficial or tangential but fascinates students can give you entrée into more essential matters, so brainstorm as many as you can.)

8. What learning dispositions should you cultivate and ask your students to pay attention to?

CHAPTER 4

Strategies for Discovery

A cross-grade team of teachers from Oulu, Finland, wanted to expand their use of inquiry as a springboard for student learning. Specifically, they wanted to encourage primary students to make observations and raise questions about what they were seeing in the world around them. Learning through observation occurs in real life, so teachers began imagining how to bring inquiry into students' daily activities—travelling to and from school, pursuing hobbies, or just spending time at home.

Finland has one of the highest per-capita uses of mobile phones in the world. That meant teachers knew their students would have ready access to mobile devices. As primary school teacher Pasi Mattila explains, "The camera phone is familiar for pupils and a meaningful tool for communicating and working. The benefit of a mobile data terminal [i.e., a mobile phone connected to other networked technologies] is that it goes where the learners go."

The Finnish teachers continued brainstorming about how to connect all the pieces of their project: instructional goals and accessible technologies, plus student collaboration and problem-solving skills. They designed a project that makes use of camera phones, GPS, and a networked learning environment called Moop to support the process of inquiry learning. Mattila calls the result "meaningful and motivating learning." In one authentic project, student teams gathered and analyzed data about recycling to make observations about recycling habits at home and in the community. They then developed recommendations for a school recycling program.

This chapter focuses on selecting and designing projects. You may decide to adapt a project plan that has been developed—and already classroom tested—by another teacher or teaching team. Or, like the creative teachers from Oulu, you might want to design your own project from scratch, integrating technology in new ways to reach your instructional goals. Either way, the same critical thinking goes into planning. By the end of the chapter, you will have worked through a process to create a basic project idea that encompasses your most important learning aims.

REVIEWING PROJECTS

If you decide to start with a project plan designed by someone else, remember *caveat emptor* ("let the buyer beware"). With a multitude of projects to choose from, you need to be aware that quality varies widely. Be selective.

Even if you ultimately decide to design your own project plan, there are benefits of reviewing other plans first. This gives you a chance to be a critical consumer. It's also an excellent activity to do with colleagues, especially if you are collaborating with teachers you don't yet know well. By reviewing existing plans together (such as those online at iEARN or Global SchoolNet), you will start to get a sense of the sorts of projects that interest your colleagues. You can also practice giving critical feedback without having to critique each other's project-planning efforts just yet.

OVERCOMING PITFALLS

How can you improve your own critical-thinking skills when it comes to reviewing project plans? Look past the "window dressing" of projects that seem appealing or make use of dazzling technologies. Instead, pay attention to the quality of the student experience. Are important learning aims addressed? Does the project plan include samples of student work, which you can also critique? Now, imagine your students doing the same project. Will students master rigorous content? Will they engage in activity that helps them become independent learners? Learn to make inquiries? Carry out effective research and make new meaning? Learn to learn from and with others? Use tools for important purposes? As you examine the work of others, you are engaging in just the kind of critical thinking and information literacy you want to see in students!

Here are a few pitfalls in project design to watch for:

- **Potential pitfall: Long on activity, short on learning outcomes.** If the project is busy and long but reaches small or lower-order learning aims, it's not worth investing your students' time—or yours. A project should be "right sized" for what it accomplishes. If students could learn as much through a brief lecture or by reading about the topic, then the project falls short. Also, look at the learning outcome. If every student product is similar, or if what students produce could be found easily in any reference material, this is an indication that the learning accomplished is lower-order, at the level of recall and understanding. The project may be limited, but it might also offer you the germ of a good idea. You might say to yourself: *This caught my attention but falls short. Where could my students and I go with this idea?*

- **Potential pitfall: Technology layered over traditional practice.** Having students research a topic on the Internet and then present it in an electronic slideshow is not a quality project—it is just a dressed-up version of a research report. Good projects focus on reaching significant learning outcomes, not merely making use of technology applications. If learning aims are lofty and technology helps your students reach them, then the integration of technology is essential to the project. As you are reviewing a project plan, consider whether technology is used to bring people together, connect students to rich data or primary sources, or provide some other way to allow students to create unique and high-quality learning products.

- **Potential pitfall: Trivial thematic units.** Picture a school where apples are a theme in the primary grades each autumn. Students paint apple pictures, count and add apples in math class, read stories about Johnny Appleseed, and even visit an orchard. Although apples are everywhere, the work is not interdisciplinary, collaborative, or especially rigorous. Thematic teaching is not necessarily project-based learning. Structured differently, an apple project might have elementary students learning about commerce, agriculture, and transportation when they research where apples in their grocery store come from. They might compare the selection in the store to preferences of the student body by interviewing the produce buyer, polling students at their school, and creating graphs to display their results.

  A thematic approach can be trivial, but it doesn't have to be. Some classes use a unifying theme for a whole year's work. Imagine how the themes *change* or *power* could be addressed repeatedly over the year through a variety of projects. Think about how a theme would unify a year's worth of projects and help students make important connections. Other quality themes to consider are *survival, justice, interdependence, designed and natural worlds,* and *chaos and order.* When examining thematic projects or creating your own, look for ways a theme elevates and connects the learning.

- **Potential pitfall: Overly scripted with many, many steps.** The best projects have students making critical decisions about their learning path. Be wary of over-prescriptive project plans that have many discrete steps. You and your students may be following a recipe that leads to limited and predictable results. That said, you may also be looking at a complicated project that's worth all those steps. Look to the description of learning objectives and student outcomes as you evaluate a plan. If students end with "cookie cutter" work products that look much the same, or if the outcomes otherwise do not justify the steps, you can probably find a better approach.

If you find a project that looks promising but comes up short, keep looking. You may be able to find another treatment of the same topic or remodel the project for more significant learning.

DESIGNING TERRIFIC PROJECTS: GETTING STARTED

By now, you and your colleagues should be getting a better idea of what to look for in a project. You're probably eager to start designing your own project or adapting a plan to meet your goals. But first, let's spend a few minutes "listening in" as experts talk about how they launch into the project design process. Where do their good project ideas come from? Think of those who have developed expertise in project-based learning as your advance scouts. They can help you find your way to your own excellent project. Sometimes, the journey involves avoiding the very pitfalls discussed above.

Canadian educator Sylvia Chard, professor emeritus of early childhood and elementary education at the University of Alberta, highlights many effective teacher-developed projects on her Project Approach Web site (www.projectapproach.org). Chard recommends "a flexible framework" to guide project design.

What's the value of flexibility? Take a look at the thinking behind "The Boat Project," developed by primary teacher Cheryl Weighill at Minchau Elementary School in Edmonton, Alberta, and previously featured on Chard's Web site. Weighill describes how the idea naturally emerged from the interests of her first- and second-grade students (Chard, 2007).

Originally, the primary team had planned a thematic unit on the topic of water. But then, on a cold winter day, the school organized a special event that caused the teachers to reconsider their plan. As a break from the chilly Canadian weather, children were invited to wear beach clothes to school. Activity centers gave children a choice of beach-related materials to explore. Weighill and her colleagues noticed that many of their students were enthralled with using blocks to make a model of a boat. As Weighill relates:

> The study of the ocean as a project was thought to be too broad and not part of these children's experiences or their real world; therefore, we discarded "the ocean" as the

project topic. But, since many of the children had begun constructing a boat out of the large blocks in the block center and interest was shown by the children through their conversation, questions, dialogue, anecdotes, and even their disagreements of how boats are constructed, the topic of "boats" was chosen for our project. As the block boat was being constructed, more and more of the children joined in to the role-playing of a boat experience. The children were interested in sharing their personal experiences and anecdotes. This was the birth of the boat project. One of the children announced, "We should build a boat, a real boat!" And so our journey began.
(as cited in S. Chard, personal communication, April 16, 2007)

Weighill's team could have stuck with their original thematic unit. Instead, they were wise enough to let students' interests and curiosity drive the learning experience. The resulting project allowed teachers to reach a number of important instructional goals, such as grade-level science standards relating to buoyancy, boats, and design; language arts goals; and using math problem solving and measurement for authentic tasks. The interdisciplinary project naturally led to activities that developed students' inquiry skills and taught them to do Internet research to answer their own questions. Throughout the seven-week project, students engaged in experiences that helped them become better at making decisions, working in teams, and providing evidence of what they had learned.

Author Diane McGrath shares some of her 21st-century project design strategies on her Web site, Project-Based Learning with Technology (http://coe.ksu.edu/pbl). A professor of Educational Computing, Design, and Online Learning at Kansas State University, McGrath (2002–2003) emphasizes the importance of getting away from traditional thinking when you begin to design a project:

> To really engage learners, you have to set up a situation in which they want to ask questions, want to learn more, need to know something they don't already know, and believe it is really important to them and, especially, to the larger community to find out. Your project will not be a lab in which students replicate what someone else has done. A good project will instead be an extended investigation in which students design the subquestions and the ways of trying to answer them because they believe in what they are doing.

What might this look like in practice? McGrath recently challenged secondary science teachers to design a project inspired by *New York Times* columnist Andrew Postman. Postman chronicles his attempt to go on an "energy diet" to reduce his household consumption of fossil fuels. McGrath suggests that teachers ask students the open-ended question: "How can my household lower our energy use by 5%? And what will it cost (in comfort, convenience, and money)?" She suggests steering students toward resources such as online energy calculators, multimedia sites about climate change, and Web resources from government agencies and environmental organizations.

Side Trip

Project Design Resources

Many experts have contributed research and effective strategies to our understanding about how to design effective projects. If you are interested in learning more about the research in this area, take a look at these resources:

- Buck Institute for Education—In operation since 1987, BIE offers project-based learning research, professional development, and a handbook on instructional design. Recently, BIE has given special attention to problem-based government and problem-based economics curriculum planning. www.bie.org

- Understanding by Design—Grant Wiggins and Jay McTighe's excellent book by the same title (second edition, Association for Supervision and Curriculum Development, 2005) has helped thousands of educators apply the process of "backward design" and learn how to frame curriculum around essential questions. The book also provides the framework for an online exchange that brings together registered users to share project ideas, use online tools, and have their plans reviewed by experts. www.ubdexchange.org

- Active Learning Practices for Schools (ALPS)—ALPS is a Web portal developed by the Harvard Graduate School of Education and Harvard's Project Zero. With free registration, users can take advantage of the Collaborative Curriculum Design Tool, which facilitates online collaboration. ALPS also links educators to education researchers, professors, and curriculum designers at Harvard. http://learnweb.harvard.edu/alps

THE BEST PROJECTS SHARE IMPORTANT FEATURES

Research-based frameworks for project design share distinguishing features. Keep these features in mind as you design your own project.

The best projects share the following qualities. They:

- are loosely designed with the possibility of different learning paths

- are generative, causing students to construct meaning

- center on a driving question or are otherwise structured for inquiry

- capture student interest through complex and compelling real-life or simulated experiences

- are realistic, and therefore cross multiple disciplines

- reach beyond school to involve others

- tap rich data or primary sources

- are structured so students learn with and from each other

- have students working as inquiring experts might

- get at 21st-century skills and literacies, including communication, project management, and technology use

- get at important learning dispositions, including persistence, risk-taking, confidence, resilience, self-reflection, and cooperation

- have students learn by doing

WHERE PROJECT IDEAS COME FROM

Good projects are everywhere. Even a classroom irritant can be the impetus for a quality project, according to a teacher who repurposed students' (disruptive) portable music players into devices for inquiry. Consider looking in the following different directions in search of project ideas. An example for each is included somewhere in this book—use them for inspiration.

- a tried-and-true project with potential for more meaningful, expressive learning (including opportunities for students to teach others what they have learned) see *Of Mice and Men,* chapter 9, p. 141

- project plans developed by and for other teachers see Global SchoolNet and iEARN, chapter 2, pp. 38–39

- news stories
  see Energy Diet, chapter 4, p. 63

- contemporary issues
  see Flat Classroom, chapter 5, pp. 88–89

- student questions or interests
  see The Boat Project, chapter 4, p. 62

- a classroom irritant put to educational use
  see iHistory, chapter 7, pp. 118–119

- a "mashup" of a great idea and a new tool
  see "Road" literature and Google Earth in Google Lit Trips, chapter 2, p. 36

Finally, keep in mind that one successful project will often lead you to another. Robert Griffin is a Canadian educator who became interested in the project approach several years ago. Griffin says:

> I was looking for learning activities that would meet the needs of tactile learners. When I began doing some collaborative projects about seven years ago, I noticed that the tactile learners became engaged using technology. Regardless of learning styles, all students began to do better when engaged with projects using technology. As I began to do more and more research on meeting the needs of students with learning difficulties, research showed authentic projects and authentic assessment benefited all students.

Now several years into using the technology-rich project approach, he can see how new opportunities grow out of previous successes. He relates:

> Everything we have done using technology projects has led to another level of projects. We began doing GrassRoots projects for Industry Canada. Students built Web sites about our community. The skills they learned doing these projects led to our first collaboration, a project involving six schools in New Brunswick themed on Antarctica. These projects led our school in becoming a member of the Network of Innovative Schools in Canada. These two projects led our school to receiving our first HP grant. The expertise teachers and students gained in these projects led to our school being chosen to participate in a research project.

Your Turn

Activity 1

DESIGN YOUR PROJECT

In the previous chapter, you established the learning objectives that are important to you and your students. Now, whether you decide to remodel a project you like or design one from scratch, plan how to put your ideas into operation by working through the following design process. At the end, write a project sketch—a short description of the project that you can share with others for critical feedback.

As you begin, remember that your project exists within a context. The school calendar, curriculum sequence, student readiness, and student interests are all factors to keep in mind as you plan.

Suggestion: Return to your individual or group project space on your wiki where you worked last. Refresh your memory about the learning framework you established at the end of chapter 3. You will bring those ideas forward as you continue planning. Start a new wiki page called "Project Sketch." Make notes as you follow these key design steps and then write a project sketch to share with others.

1. Revisit the framework.

   a. Make a final list of learning objectives for core subjects and allied disciplines.

   b. Decide on the specific 21st-century skills you want to address. (Think about skills that fit in these broad categories outlined in the refreshed NETS•S: creativity and innovation; communication and collaboration; research and information fluency; critical thinking, problem solving, and decision making; digital citizenship; and technology operations and concepts. In addition, consider how you will address project management skills.)

   c. Identify learning dispositions you want to foster, such as persistence and reflection.

2. Establish evidence of understanding. Imagine what students would know or be able to do once they have learned. Imagine how they would be different as learners and as people. (You will design evaluation tools later, but look ahead to chapter 9 for ideas.)

3. Plan the "vehicle" (the project theme or challenge). Think: What would students inquire about, do, create? Strive for "optimal ambiguity"—that is, both enough structure and enough flexibility to serve the needs of the project. Remember the many project examples you have read about so far. Imagine the true-to-life connections. Imagine ways experts (historians, economists, mathematicians, psychologists, engineers, doctors) interact with the topics you identified.

4. Plan entrée into the project experience. What are the first things you might say to get students' attention and build excitement for the learning ahead? What will captivate your students?

At this point your project is coming into view, but it still may be a bit blurry around the edges and lack detail. Great! If you were to design down to the last action right now, you might constrain the project and limit where students could take it. Consider the following metaphor for planning:

> Planning a student-centered project is like planning a voyage across uncharted seas. You have a destination in mind, but not knowing your route, you and your students build a trusty ship, and, bringing all your seamanship to bear, get wind in your sails and set off. It helps to have a clear picture of your destination so you'll recognize it when you see it!
> (Krauss, 1998)

Also, if you go too far you may become overly wedded to your ideas. Let planning be an iterative and collaborative process. Get feedback on your ideas from your colleagues. Revise and rework your plan a few times. Your project will be better for the effort.

You may be anticipating next steps, including designing learning tasks, preparation, guiding the learning, and evaluation. These will be addressed in the next chapter. For now, sum up the plan so far in a project sketch.

WRITE A PROJECT SKETCH

Pause here and write a project sketch—a brief account of your project. A project sketch is a light, quick treatment, not a painting that captures every detail. The project sketch is a synthesis of what you have thought about so far. Describe the project in a paragraph. Give it a title if that gets your ideas flowing. Write it again from another angle.

Flesh out the picture just enough so you can share it with peers and get critical feedback.

Here is a project sketch to get your thoughts flowing:

Sample Project Sketch: Travel U.S.A.
In fifth-grade social studies, we study the regions of the U.S. My idea is to make this study more substantial. Instead of just doing a research report, students will compare, analyze, and decide for themselves what is significant about a region. My fifth-graders are going to form "travel agencies" and prepare an informative and persuasive proposal for a foreign family deciding on a U.S. vacation. Each "agency" makes decisions about the most important things to know, places to visit, and activities to do in their assigned region, taking into account the interests and cultural backgrounds of their visitors. They will have to establish their own criteria for what is significant, and I will guide them. Along the way, students read travel blogs and Web sites, find and interview people who live in or have visited the target region, ask a real local travel agent to work with them, research airfare and other travel information, "meet" people online from the originating country to learn about culture and possible likes and dislikes, and read and recommend literature about the region. Their products will include sample itineraries, a travel budget, and marketing materials such as brochures. They will create informative and persuasive proposals and make "pitches" to other students, who will act as critical "clients." In this way, all students learn about all the regions from each other. Students might choose different technologies for the project—for example, a podcast "walking tour" through a historic district, or a multimedia slideshow or film travelogue showing a sample "tour." The products and presentations will vary depending on interest, but a rubric will define core learning outcomes and guide their work. I expect this project to last three weeks. Students will work on it three times a week in class for an hour and also outside of school.

Share your project sketches with your colleagues. Together, ask hard questions and suggest ways to make each project better. Imagine how it might become more comprehensive or realistic. Think of ways to capture students' interests and involve other teachers, school specialists, or professionals in the community. Imagine the paths of inquiry teams might take as they make the project their own. Give each project a name.

Your Turn

Activity 2: Create an Asset Map

An asset map is an inventory of the material goods, strengths, and talents of the people who make up a team, organization, or community. Build a visual map of your assets in order to bring resources, knowledge, skills, and capacities out into the open where they can be used for everyone's benefit. Through this exercise, you will build a lasting artifact to remind you of the abundance around you.

If you are creating a project on your own, complete this activity alone and then get input from others. If your team is working on a collaborative project, the activity is the perfect way to inventory your assets for reference as you start your collaboration.

Directions: On a large sheet of chart paper or on a whiteboard, create a large diagram with a circle in the center that says "Project Assets." On spokes leading out from the center write these words: *Ourselves, Students, Others*, and *Resources*. Start with *Ourselves* by asking the following: *What special capabilities do we have among ourselves? What skills, talents, and interests do we express inside and outside of work that may be useful in this project?* Write names around the "Ourselves" spoke. Add assets next to them. If people share qualities, connect the qualities with a line.

A finished "Ourselves" spoke might say:

> Mark—organizer, social studies, community connector, knows historians
> & service orgs, task management; Maribel—writer/blogger, creative, multi-
> media, Web tools (esp. Flickr), persuasive, music; Jody—curriculum + pbl
> expert, imagineer, knows arts council, music, traveler; Mitchell—tech sup-
> port, Web desktops, tutorials, organizer, tech-finder, athletic; John—math,
> sports, recording, local history/issues, connects with hard-to-engage kids,
> foodie, handy with tools.

Extend the reach of this spoke by including adjunct staff and volunteers in
your school.

What capabilities do kids have? Think about their skills, talents, and, interests inside and outside of school. The "Students" spoke might say: "artsy class,
media talents, dramatic (some even in drama), 7–10 talented musicians, all
manage work on server, 90% use chat, most have cell phones, many multi-
taskers, tech club=25, 50% social networking, 30%? used to projects. Interest
in enviro = high. JK/SB/AP=tech leadership; MB/HH/JL/MP= projects."

Continue with this process for "Others." List people who have assets that will
support a successful project. They might include school personnel, parents, a
staff member's spouse, the mayor, a local business owner, a historian, a professional you know, a professional you don't know, people near and virtually near,
older students, a blogging expert, someone who knows someone who knows
someone—you get the idea. Don't forget the expanding pool of retired educators who can help! Write the capabilities of each "Other" as he or she relates to
the project. Capabilities might include "expert in medicine," "can teach a mini-
course," "has performance space," "knows older people w/ time," "knows Java,"
"can build blog," "fundraising/publicity exp.," "interested in youth," "should
know about this project," and so on. Add more paper or space if you need it.

Now think about resources. These are the material goods, spaces, and time
you might put to use. This section might look something like the following:
"37 networked computers (20—lab, 5—teacher desktop, 3–4 each class),
11 non-networked computers (old) 1 color printer, 4 b&w printers; peripherals: 1 smartboard and projector, webinar software, server with student space,
student e-mail accounts, public library computers 4–9 pm, meeting space

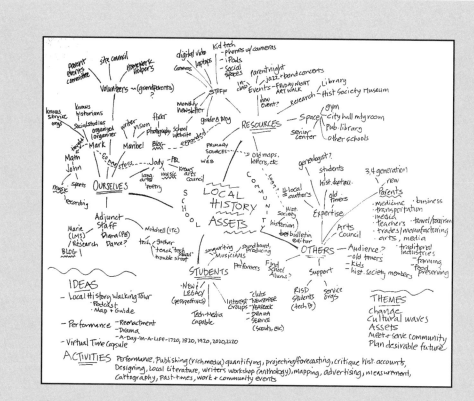

Figure 3 Asset mapping reveals the resources and talents a team can put to use for a project.

before & after school, wiki space not being used, parent group funding (up to $150), 5–6 parent volunteers (more in evening), annual community day—June, weekly principal report, monthly family newsletter, Mark's blog, 90-minute block schedule, Wednesday integrated period 180 minutes." Figure 3 shows how this sample asset map would look at this stage.

After you create your asset map, hang it in a common space so team members can continue adding to it. Paper maps work well, but technology can help you share the map with a wider audience. If you used a white board, you can capture a digital image of your map and share it online. Or, you might consider making your map using a collaborative concept mapping tool such as bubbl.us (http://bubbl.us), so that others can continue adding new ideas.

Refer to the map from time to time, and put the information to work as you involve others and identify more assets. Show them *this* map and ask them to add on. Finally, if you need more support, survey the community to unearth hidden assets. Conduct the poll using a survey created with an online tool such as SurveyMonkey. Describe the project and get people excited when you send out the survey link. Make sure the survey is open-ended enough that people can find many ways to participate, perhaps even in ways you have not anticipated.

LEARN ABOUT ASSET MAPPING

Asset mapping began as a community development process. To learn more, see the following resources:

- Asset-Based Community Development Institute— http://www.northwestern.edu/ipr/abcd.html

- *Mapping Community Assets Workbook*—Available for free download from the Northwest Regional Educational Laboratory at http://www.nwrel.org/ruraled/publications/com_mapping.pdf.

Technology Focus

Track Assets Online

As your project comes together, consider using technical aids to help you manage your bountiful assets and resources. A simple, sortable spreadsheet table may suffice, but don't let it live on a desktop. Upload or build your spreadsheet in an online, Web-based space that will give everyone on your team access in order to add and manage assets. A spreadsheet will help you track not only specific skills ("knows about astronomy") and resources ("digital video equipment"), but also useful information such as phone numbers and e-mail addresses. Consider how you might leverage this activity into a bigger resource for your school community. For example, parents from previous years might be willing to continue sharing their expertise as their children move on to new grades. Imagine what a gift it would be to welcome a new teacher with access to your online assets survey!

Examples of Web-based spreadsheet applications include the following:

- Google Docs. Take an online tour of this Web-based resource at www.google.com/google-d-s/intl/en/tour1.html.

- Zoho Creator (http://creator.zoho.com) is an online database manager. At its simplest, Zoho Creator functions like a stripped-down version of Microsoft Access. Use it to turn spreadsheets into online databases to share with others. You can also use it to build Web forms for others to fill out and then manage the returned data. Consider asking the larger community to reflect on the assets they might contribute to your project by creating a survey and sharing it through Zoho.

CHAPTER 5

Project Management Strategies for Teachers and Learners

Managing a project requires a 21st-century set of skills. In the business world, a good project manager is a masterful communicator, an efficient time manager, a careful budgeter, and a tireless troubleshooter. These skills can be applied to the world of teaching and learning, too. When you become a successful manager of digital-age projects, you draw on a combination of skills to facilitate your students' learning. What's more, your students learn from your example. Before long, they will begin developing their own strategies for managing their time, collaborating with team members, assessing their progress, and maximizing their learning experiences.

In previous chapters, you started thinking about the project planning process. By now, you have considered the big ideas that you want your students to explore, have mapped these to standards, and are starting to envision how the project could unfold. Pull up your project wiki and make notes as you are prompted to think about how you and your students will manage your efforts to make the most of the learning opportunities ahead.

Thoughtful preparation will benefit you and your students, regardless of the scale of the project you are planning. You may be starting with a small project, joining an already existing project, or planning a more complex project that will unfold over several weeks. Whatever the scope, you want to make the best use of your time—and your students'.

This chapter helps you invest your time wisely on the "front-loaded" part of design—before you ever engage students in project work. The first part of the chapter prompts you to consider the resources you will need and to plan strategies to support effective time management, teaming, and assessment. By considering these important topics in advance of project launch, you ensure that you are ready to make the best use of instructional time once the project is underway. At the end of the chapter, the focus shifts to the ways you and your students can use technology to manage projects and maximize learning potential.

Side Trip

Be Resourceful

Keeping your project within budget is a 21st-century skill. In some communities, online clearinghouses help connect teachers with the (free) materials they need. For example, Portland, Oregon, is home to SCRAP, the School and Community Reuse Action Project. This nonprofit organization diverts thousands of pounds of reusable materials from the waste stream to the hands of teachers. An outreach program includes workshops to show teachers how to incorporate reusable materials into environmental and art projects and other uses. Learn more at www.scrapaction.org.

Use craigslist, too, or another online community network with free classified ads. Browse for the materials or services you need or post a want ad of your own.

GATHERING RESOURCES: WHAT (AND WHO) WILL YOU NEED?

In the last chapter, you made an asset map, an inventory of resources in your school and extended learning community. Perhaps you used an online tool to inventory the skills, tools, expertise, and other community resources available to you and your students, and loaded information into a database. Now that you are preparing to launch a specific project, it's time to gather the resources you will need. Take another look at your assets inventory and consider how specific resources could support this project.

What materials will you need? Take a look at your inventory and see what supplies, tools, or other materials are available at school or offered by your parent community and other supporters. If you don't find what you need, put out the word about your upcoming project. Use your class Web site or an e-mail newsletter to parents to post a wish list of supplies. Don't overlook other community resources, such as local recycling centers, as potentially excellent sources of supplies.

Will your project involve the use of technologies that are new to you or your students? Refer back to chapter 3 and think about the essential learning functions you need technology to deliver, and then select the tools that will help students meet the learning goals. Plan for the introduction of unfamiliar tools (look ahead to chapter 6 for many ways to do this).

Will you need to expand your students' access to technology? Think creatively about how to make access more frequent and equitable. Cecilia Mag-isa Estoque, a teacher from the Caraga Region of the Philippines, faced high barriers to access when she set out to create a collaborative online literacy project with a teacher from Manila. Estoque's high school has only one computer lab for some 9,000 students. She involved the local community by establishing partnerships with owners of the Internet cafés near her school in Butuan City. For a small fee of 10 pesos, teams of students were able to have frequent computer and Internet access during the project, which she called "My Personal Encounter with the Little Prince."

Will your students need access to experts to answer the questions that are apt to come up during your project? Consider ways to engage with experts both in person and from a distance. For example, you might invite an expert to give a live demonstration that is relevant to the project. One elementary teacher enlisted the help of a student's mother, who worked in a forensics lab, during a project modeled on the popular television series, *CSI.* Another invited a student's father, a physician, to dissect a fish during an integrated study involving salmon.

Experts aren't always available to pay a personal visit to your classroom, but technology can bring them closer. A high school teacher who has students design their own research projects never knows in advance which topics his students will choose to investigate. One year, a student team might want to interview an archaeologist. Another year, a team will need to pose questions to a child psychologist or sociologist. This teacher continues to expand his database of experts. As questions arise, he can direct students to experts who are willing to mentor them via e-mail.

Similarly, videoconferencing and virtual field trips can help bridge the distance between your students and the experts who work in the disciplines they are studying. A high school physiology teacher uses videoconferencing to enable her students to watch surgeries—in real time. Her students prepare diligently before a scheduled surgery, when they are able to not only observe, but also ask questions of the surgical team. In another community, a team of elementary teachers schedules virtual field trips to "take" their rural students to art museums, observatories, and other places they cannot readily travel.

Who else can help with your project? Don't overlook the technology coordinator, media specialist, and other specialists in your district. For starters, they can help your students learn discrete skills, such as setting up Web sites or performing research online. They may also be able to support more sophisticated project activities, such as students creating multimedia presentations or videos to document their results. Make a point of getting to know these specialists. Include them during project planning and take advantage of their expertise.

Cecilia Mag-isa Estoque, the Philippines teacher who designed the Little Prince project, asked the specialists at her school computer lab to conduct an introductory session for her students at the start of the project. The students had a three-hour introduction in the lab, including time to set up individual Web-based e-mail accounts, which they needed to communicate with distant students. Later, when they were working on their projects at a neighborhood Internet café, the owner gave them more instruction in using Web publishing to share their projects online.

If you are collaborating with a teaching team, think about how you will divide responsibilities. What are your individual strengths and interests? For which tasks will each of you be responsible? How will you organize who does what when? Look back at the skills, talents, and interests area of your asset map to remind yourselves what you are good at and what you like.

MILESTONES AND DEADLINES: IT'S ABOUT TIME

Teaching students to become effective managers of their own time should be an overarching goal of any project; this is a skill that will support them throughout their education and beyond. Projects of all sizes offer opportunities to teach and reinforce good time management skills.

Plan a project calendar with milestones along the way. Your students' attention to time management will be better if you share a project calendar that makes deadlines visual. Use an online calendar or time line tool, or take the low-tech route and simply use a magnetic calendar with a moving marker. Either way, a good project calendar will help students see the deadlines of upcoming milestones so they can plan ahead, track their own progress, and troubleshoot potential delays before they fall behind.

If you are planning a project that lasts several weeks, chunk big tasks into smaller, more manageable pieces. Make sure students are aware of the smaller deadlines they will need to meet along the way.

Share your planning calendar with parents, too. A class Web site, project blog, or weekly e-mail about the project will allow you to communicate with parents about upcoming deadlines and milestones.

Learning management systems offer teachers and students another way to organize all the components of a project in an online environment. At New Technology High School, for example, teachers load all the components of a project online. Each student has a personal briefcase where project work is stored. This secure online space is accessible from any computer connected to the Internet, allowing students to work on projects at school, at home, at the library, or elsewhere in the community. Teachers can see student work while it is in progress, giving them opportunities to answer questions, resolve confusion, and provide formative assessment throughout the project. (See Technology Focus: Project Management with Technology, page 84, to learn more about setting up an online project space.)

TEAM PLANNING

How will student teams be organized? Carmel Crane, a New Technology teacher who has used the project approach for years, says students naturally gravitate "to the kids they feel most comfortable with." She acknowledges the importance of "good chemistry," but also steps in to mix up the teams regularly. "You want students who will complement each others' attributes," she says. "One student might be better at organizing, while another is good at using technology. A good team needs a mix of skills. I make sure to switch the groups around for the next project so they get experience working with different people."

In your role as project manager, you need to remember that students will be doing different things at different times. Sometimes, individuals will work alone on separate parts of a team effort. Other times, team members will be working together. As project manager, you will be supporting students who are going about the many activities that a project involves.

The team approach requires you to reset your expectations and experiment with different combinations. Students will sometimes work separately, other times in pairs or small groups, and occasionally will come together as a whole class. In these shifting contexts, how will you ensure that all students are challenged? How will you meet special learning needs? How will you ensure that students take seriously their responsibility for the team's success? In some situations, you may want to team students who share a certain skill, proficiency, or interest. Other times, you may want to mix students whose strengths complement one another.

Michael McDowell, a biology teacher at New Technology High School, believes that managing student teams is critical to the success of project-based learning. At his school, student teams work out a contract at the start of any project. They agree to language that describes the responsibilities of each team member as well as the consequences of letting down the team. Contracts even spell out what it would take for a student to be fired from the team.

When McDowell plans a project, he takes into consideration how he will assess team dynamics. "I want to assess not just their content, but how they are working as a group," he says. In particular, he wants to be sure one overachiever is not carrying the load. "Early on, I look at things like commitment: Are all students engaged? Are they appreciating each other? Do they have clear and objective goals? Is their contract explicit and understood by all?"

Team management takes effort, but McDowell insists it's worth the investment. "If a team works well together, they're going to accomplish things they never thought they could do."

Spotlight

Teams That Maximize Results

When Julie Lindsay and Vicki Davis set up their Flat Classroom Project, they thought hard about how to match up student teams from Bangladesh and the U.S. Davis describes their team planning process:

> We worked hard to match students well. Most worked in pairs (one student from each school). Julie and I didn't have a set way to match them, but we looked for things that would make a good fit, like a common interest. We wanted to make sure they would work with somebody who would challenge them and augment their strengths. We talked through our classes and gave this a lot of thought. In a more typical cooperative project, the teacher often puts a stronger student with a weaker one. And the stronger one often

does more of the work. We wanted students to be somewhat comparable in abilities. We didn't want one student to carry the other. We were looking for growth as individuals. They don't grow if they sit and watch someone else do everything for them. We looked at their learning styles and their strengths. You might have one student who is strong at writing matched with another who excels at creating video, and who is a very auditory learner. Together, they would make a more complete team. If you take two who are alike, they may not see the whole picture.

Matching teams wasn't easy to do, especially with students from different cultures. But we felt strongly that we didn't want any student to have an excuse not to perform. All of our students were able to complete the project, but some really high-achieving students wanted to do a world-class job. They liked being matched with a teammate who had a similar quest for excellence. They found kindred spirits, and that was nice.

PLAN FOR ASSESSMENT

How do you know what prior knowledge and interests your students bring to a project? How will you discover and clear up student misunderstandings or help students learn from setbacks? How can you encourage students to build on what they have learned and push for even deeper understanding? Assessment is an integral part of project-based learning. With planning and practice, you can take advantage of assessment opportunities throughout the project—not just at the end. Formative assessment will create more opportunities to know what your students are thinking and understanding, so that you can better facilitate successful learning. Paying attention to assessment will also help you think broadly about how well this project works. How will you know that it has been a successful learning journey?

In their landmark international study, Paul Black and Dylan Wiliam describe formative assessment as the feature found at the heart of effective teaching (Black & Wiliam, 1998). While acknowledging that formative assessment includes a wide range of activities, from quizzes to conversation to written reflection, they stress the benefits of assessment when it is used to adapt teaching to meet student needs.

A complex project requires multiple assessment methods, ranging from formal to informal evaluations. Author Lois Bridges counts at least five categories of assessment, each involving different teacher behaviors. *Monitoring* involves the use of checklists, inventories, or project logs to assess student progress. *Observing* means watching and listening to what students do and say. *Interacting* requires asking questions to coax students into deeper thinking. *Analyzing* involves collecting and analyzing artifacts of student learning. *Reporting* means organizing performance data to share with students, parents, and others (Bridges, 1996).

Spotlight

Just-in-Time Feedback

A California high school journalism teacher named Esther Wojcicki has her students use a shared online workspace for all their writing. The technology, called Google Docs, allows her to give students immediate feedback. "Sometimes, I'll notice in the opening paragraph that they are off track or have omitted important information. I can make a comment right in the text. That gets them back on track right away, before they get too far down the wrong road," she explains.

Wojcicki says the online collaborative tool has changed the way she teaches by creating new opportunities for formative assessment. "Before, it was too chaotic in the computer lab for me to give students any real-time feedback," she says. "They would be asking questions—help me with this, how do I do that. There was no time to review what they were writing, so I would wait until they finished a draft before I gave feedback. Now, I can help them earlier in the process. They can make revisions in a flash and move on."

Wojcicki contrasts her current approach with a more traditional English class, "where you write an essay and get it back three weeks later. By then, it's too late to fix anything." She explains, "That's disheartening, and it doesn't teach you the process of repetitive revising. That's how you improve as a writer."

Because the Google workspace is accessible from any connected computer, Wojcicki is able to keep up-to-date with her students at all times. "I was away from class for a few days to attend a conference, and my freshmen had a substitute helping them write an introduction," she says. "I could see what they were doing as they were doing it."

Her more advanced students learn to critique each other's writing. Collaborating online, they provide one another with critical feedback—even at odd hours. "Sometimes, I overhear that students were working together until midnight. They see each other's work as it's happening," she explains, "and that has a huge impact on they way they interact. They get very good at providing feedback, and they seem to take suggestions more seriously when they come from their peers." On the drafts she receives, Wojcicki can review the many comments and edits suggested by critical peers.

Palo Alto High School's award-winning student newspaper and magazine are evidence of the high quality work that students are capable of producing. "Nothing is more effective for improving writing than peer critique," says the veteran adviser. "These students are writing for an authentic audience, so they are motivated. The feedback is live, online, quick, and from their peers. They learn fast." To read the newspaper, go to Palo Alto High publications online at http://www.paly.net/publications.php.

Technology can support a range of assessment activities. For example, an online survey can help you assess what students know as they come into a project. What is their readiness level? Do they have prior experience that relates to content areas, technology, or project work in general? Would they benefit from building some discrete skills before launching into the project?

The project planning stage is your opportunity to design tools to help you assess student progress and performance. For example, scoring rubrics will help you focus assessment on specific categories, such as content knowledge, discrete skills, or dispositions (such as independent work habits, collaboration, effort, or use of time). Online rubric generators, such as Rubistar (http://rubistar.4teachers.org) or Intel Education's Assessing Projects tool (http://educate.intel.com/en/AssessingProjects), allow you to create and store a custom rubric to suit your project requirements or adopt rubrics that other teachers have designed. Rubrics help you focus your attention on desired outcomes. They also help communicate learning goals and degrees of accomplishment to students.

By planning to incorporate student reflection activities throughout a project, you encourage students to practice self-assessment. Assessing their own work helps students identify their strengths and weaknesses, and ensures that they understand the learning goals you are working toward together. By making self-assessment a habit, students get the message that they can continue to improve and grow in understanding. For example, Michael McDowell frequently asks students to consider how they might "go beyond the rubric." He explains, "I encourage them to show me that they can innovate by producing learning outcomes I have not even imagined."

In teaching, as in other disciplines, effective project management involves minimizing risks—but also maximizing opportunities.

Technology Focus

Project Management with Technology

Managing complex projects is the stuff of real work. Students need project management skills and technical support structures in order to grapple with the rich and complicated nature of projects. Teachers as team coordinators, enabling advisers, and evaluators need systems that make their work and communications more manageable, too. Digital tools can support teachers in the high-level orchestration of projects and students as they get into the messy but meaningful business of learning through projects.

TEACHERS' PROJECT-MANAGEMENT NEEDS

The project-management tools and strategies teachers need include:

- tools for communicating with students and others about the project
- tools for making milestones and events visible and for notifying students when changes occur
- methods for getting resources to students
- systems for managing work products

- structures that support a productive learning environment in which teams and individuals are engaged in a variety of learning tasks at the same time

- assessment tools and strategies, including:

  o ways to gauge whether students are working productively and accomplishing project goals

  o ways to assess the load balance within a team so no individuals end up doing too much or too little

  o ways to give just-in-time feedback on student work as it develops, not just when it's completed

STUDENTS' PROJECT-MANAGEMENT NEEDS

The project-management tools and strategies students need include:

- systems and tools that help them manage their time and flow of work

- systems that help students manage materials and control work drafts

- collaboration tools

- methods for seeking assistance

- ways to get and use feedback on their work, through self-reflection, team input, and teacher advice

- ways to work iteratively and to see how parts add up to the whole

There are a number of ways you can meet these complex needs. The best solution for your project will depend on what ready-made resources and technical support you have at hand, as well as your own comfort level for innovating with technologies that require some "do-it-yourself" set up.

START WITH AVAILABLE TOOLS

The most basic tool for managing projects may be a district server, where a teacher sets up project folders in which students store and manage work files. While at school, students can get to their work from any networked computer. This is a simple way to manage files, but some schools block outside access, students cannot collaborate on work products with remote contributors or work with their materials away from school. To help students create and manage their work, "mash up" use of the district server with other tools described below.

Teachers and students in a school with a learning management system (LMS) can use many of its functions to manage projects. (An LMS is a software package that enables the delivery of learning content and resources to students with class management, grading, assignment drop boxes, and other functions. Several examples are Moodle and Interact, which are open-source applications, and Desire2Learn and Angel Learning, which are commercial software.)

An LMS can serve as the portal and repository for projects. In it, teachers can post time lines, resources, and assignments, and collect and grade work. Students can usually get to their work from outside of school when it's housed in an LMS. They can view calendars, discuss work with teammates through threaded discussion or chat, and download and upload work products.

For example, the technology "backbone" for the New Technology Foundation's network of schools is a customized version of Lotus Notes, Domino, and LearningSpace software. (See chapter 1, Spotlight: The New Technology Model, page 15. Along with integrated e-mail, calendaring, and other collaboration tools, New Tech schools use a custom "project briefcase" as the main organizational tool for any classroom. For each project a teacher designs, he or she uploads associated documents, assignments, presentations, and rubrics to the briefcase. The project briefcase becomes the primary way students interact with the curriculum. During their years at a New Technology Foundation high school, each student amasses a body of work in a personal electronic portfolio.

A 10th-grade student from New Technology High School in Napa, California, describes using Lotus Notes: "Once you get the hang of it, you just glide along." He says, "The briefcase is like a project planner. All the information is there. I can e-mail my teachers and get a quick response. If I need to meet with them, we schedule a time using the calendar feature."

If you are comfortable with your school's LMS, it offers a clear choice for managing a project. But, without wholesale adoption by a school or district and robust technical support, many teachers find the configuration and management of their LMS challenging and time-consuming. Also, depending on the specific package, it may be difficult for collaborators outside the school to participate in work products being developed in the system. When using an LMS, consider adding Web-based tools, such as the ones described below, that support collaboration and other project management functions.

WEB-BASED APPLICATIONS

Consider selecting from an assortment of Web-based applications and services to suit the needs of your project. There are several ways to go. You can link a set of tools together in a wiki, associate them with a blog, or alternatively, use a Web-based "desktop" application.

A wiki at its simplest is an easily edited Web page. Users create pages of sharable content using just a browser and the most basic markup language to format text, add Web links, or build new pages. Collaborators can write and edit together, from anywhere. A wiki can be open to anyone or limited by password. Wiki pages can be syndicated so collaborators or readers can learn about new content as it changes. Wikis maintain a version history, so if something goes wrong, users can revert to an earlier version. (In addition, teachers can examine version histories to gauge activity and collaboration.) Many collaborators use a wiki to write together and then pull the contents off the wiki to publish in another form (as the authors of this book did when drafting the manuscript). Wikis are great tools for developing information that flows from many to many. Wikispaces and PBwiki are two wikis popularly used in education.

A blog is an easily edited Web page, too, but in structure and flow it is more of a one-to-many delivery system, with one primary author controlling the contents. Viewers can comment on postings made by the author, but interaction in a blog is less of a free-for-all than in a wiki. A blog offers a great tool for communicating about progress or milestones and to broadcast news related to the project. Additionally, you can create separate blogs for your students to publish in and link them to your own blog. As students write in their blogs, you can keep publishing control in your hands, and help them decide when their work is ready for debut on the Web.

Drupal (http://drupal.org) and Textpattern (http://textpattern.com) are more sophisticated Web spaces that combine a content management framework and blogging engine. Highly configurable, with plugins such as discussion forums and surveys, these open-source systems offer many functions for Web collaboration. (Drupal carries the tagline "Community plumbing.") One example of Drupal used for student work and for presenting a school's face to the world is the Meriwether Lewis Elementary School site at http://lewis elementary.org.

START SIMPLY, THEN ELABORATE

The simplest way to begin using the Web to support projects may be to build a project wiki. You can construct a main project page with announcements and links and build several team pages. In these associated pages your students can communicate with you and build more pages as they collaborate with others. Before long you may have a wiki that links to a blog your class uses to share the project with others.

To imagine the possibilities, examine the high-functioning wiki that supports the Flat Classroom Project at http://flatclassroomproject.wikispaces.com.

In their two-week Flat Classroom Project, students in Bangladesh and Georgia paired up to explain, explore, and discuss topics from Thomas Friedman's *The World is Flat*. Their teachers set up a wiki that serves as the meeting place and workspace for all aspects of the project. One of the collaborating teachers, Vicki Davis of Camilla, Georgia, describes her use of wikis in the blog she authors, Cool Cat Teacher: "For classroom organization, the wiki is my hub. I guess you could say, I have a wiki-centric classroom. Whether it is blogs, podcasts, wikis, or vodcasts, if it is created in my classroom, it is linked on the wiki. If the student creates it, they are to link it. It gives us one place to organize and post and one place to send content to me." (2006, Aug. 24)

The Flat Classroom wiki is teeming with great functions, including:

- audio introductions from the teachers and students to each other
- links to resource pages that support the project, including (to name a few) a resources list, screencast tutorials, and a code of ethics for two schools working together
- external links especially relating to *The World is Flat*
- photographs of students in each class
- clocks showing the times in Bangladesh and Georgia, U.S.A. (helpful for planning collaboration across the globe)

- a link to each class's Flickr site with project photos

- updates from the teachers, including a reminder of an international call between the classes

- voice-over IP (computer-to-computer) conference calling with Skype

- links to student project blogs with multimedia

- RSS feeds so students are aware of project updates as they happen

- a ClustrMap showing Web visits from viewers around the world and over time

Davis appreciates the wiki as a place to hold all student artifacts, no matter where they were created. "Students were creating digital artifacts all over the Web for this project. We encouraged them to use whatever tool is appropriate to express their message," she explains. "The wiki does a beautiful job of marking exactly who has done what. You can quantify, in precise detail, what each person contributes to the project."

PERSONALIZED WEB PAGES

It is now possible for your students to build their own virtual offices on the Web, configured with the spaces and tools they need to manage research, create work products, and share what they are doing with others. Variously referred to as "home pages," "desktops," and "startpages," these personalized offices support an assortment of handy tools including Web mail, calendars, notepads, and news and blog feeds, to name just a few. Netvibes, Protopage, Pageflakes, iGoogle, and My Yahoo! are some of the virtual office providers.

Students participating in the Flat Classroom Project in the Bangladesh school used Protopage for their personal desktops, while their Georgia counterparts used Netvibes. In the Bangladesh school, a student team created a Protopage desktop with multiple "tabbed" pages (including one supplied by their teacher), each with an assortment of Web 2.0 tools, links, images, and work products.

The Bangladesh desktop (as shown in figure 4) shows the top of a stack of tabbed pages on one team's desktop. The page on top is one that teacher Julie Lindsay made and shared with all teams. It contains Web tools and resources she wants everyone to have, each in its own sticky-note style "block" or "widget." These elements include a teacher-created block of text advising "How to discuss and weigh up an issue," a list of topical news feeds, a set of links to class blogs, and more. Her shared page becomes a key element of each team's desktop. The rest of the tabbed pages are built by the team, and they represent the

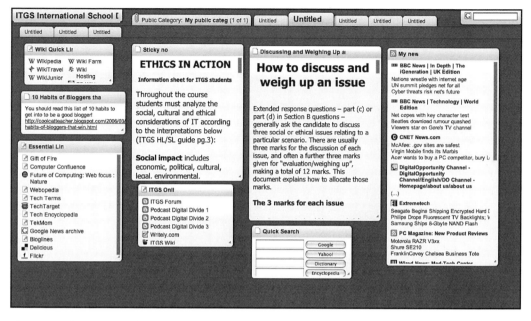

Figure 4 The top page of a "stack" of Protopage populated with selected tools and resources. This page was distributed by the teacher to all teams.

team's own organizational logic. In this example, the desktop is organized with tabbed pages for more tools, snippets of research, podcasting resources, team photos, and portfolio items.

The Georgia school used Netvibes, which also allows page sharing. Netvibes works well in schools with firewalls. If a school prohibits a particular Web site (such as MySpace), that application can be disallowed while leaving others available for use.

If you wish students to set up desktops like these, build a tabbed page with information and tool blocks you want everyone to have and share that page with students. Limit the blocks on that page to those that serve the project management and research functions you imagine all students will need. Beyond this, let students create the rest of the pages by figuring out which tools and organizational styles serve them best (more 21st-century thinking!). Your basic requirement should be that the tools support their learning. If you look at a desktop and it doesn't make sense to you, ask the student to explain how it functions for him or her. Students' selection and arrangement of tools and information is really a window into their thinking about the project. If they cannot explain their organizational structure, then they are probably confused, too.

The ever-expanding array of options need not be overwhelming. Jeff Whipple, technology mentor in New Brunswick, says matching tools and kids is easy: "Let them choose. Give them a platform where they can be creative and work together. That's more important than the particular tools they choose."

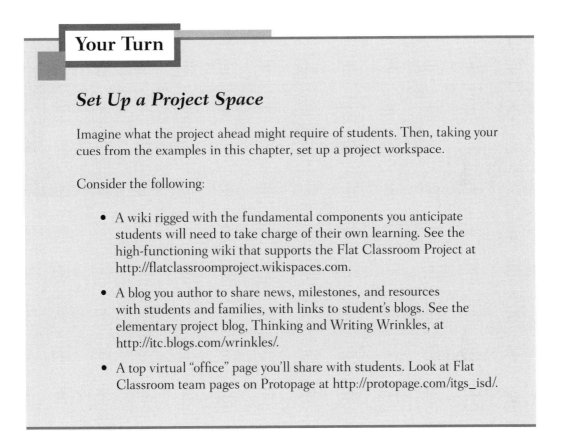

Your Turn

Set Up a Project Space

Imagine what the project ahead might require of students. Then, taking your cues from the examples in this chapter, set up a project workspace.

Consider the following:

- A wiki rigged with the fundamental components you anticipate students will need to take charge of their own learning. See the high-functioning wiki that supports the Flat Classroom Project at http://flatclassroomproject.wikispaces.com.

- A blog you author to share news, milestones, and resources with students and families, with links to student's blogs. See the elementary project blog, Thinking and Writing Wrinkles, at http://itc.blogs.com/wrinkles/.

- A top virtual "office" page you'll share with students. Look at Flat Classroom team pages on Protopage at http://protopage.com/itgs_isd/.

Section III

Navigating the Learning Experience

Section III focuses on the critical stage when your project shifts from plan to action. From project launch through the implementation phase, maximize learning potential by effectively using classroom discussions, assessment, and technology tools.

CHAPTER 6

Project Launch—
Implementation Strategies

Project kickoff is the start of a deep, thoughtful learning cycle. Take time to inspire interest and learn what students already know and care about. Teach prerequisite concepts or skills (including those relating to technology) that students need for their projects. The beginning of a project is the time to fill students with optimism and curiosity about their journey into the learning ahead.

LAYING THE GROUNDWORK

During projects, students will inquire, study, plan, evaluate, compare, collaborate, manage, create, and present. They will try new tools and help others use the ones they know. They will organize their work over time and reshape work products into more polished forms. They will give constructive feedback and respond to feedback from others. Sometimes they will work independently, and at other times, in groups. They will ask questions and present what they know. They will feel frustration and accomplishment. They will evaluate the success of their efforts, change direction, and persist as they overcome obstacles. Through the project and all of its cognitive demands, they will become more experienced, and they will be more capable learners at the end.

Before and after a project, have students complete a self-evaluation that focuses on the learning dispositions you expect them to develop during the project. The act of self-assessment causes students to think about their capabilities and how they direct their own learning. Throughout the project, as you ask students to think about their thinking and processes, they will become more aware and articulate about their metacognitive strategies. At the end of the project, when they reflect on their capabilities again, students will be able to identify specific experiences and activities that helped them grow. They will feel a deserved sense of accomplishment and be all the more ready to tackle the next challenging project.

As students gain experience in project-based learning, lay out projects in broad strokes, and help students establish their own goals and standards of excellence. Consider building an operational definition for quality by building rubrics or scoring checklists together. This offers yet one more opportunity to build awareness of the skills and attitudes of accomplished scholars.

Technology tools can encourage students to be reflective and evaluate their own strengths. For example:

- Blogs offer students space where they can reflect over time about what they are learning.

- ProfilerPRO (www.profilerpro.com) is an online survey tool that allows you to identify the learning characteristics of an individual and also among members of a group. You can identify interests, strengths, and weaknesses, and use this information as you guide learning. Create your own survey in ProfilerPRO or adapt a template to meet your needs. You can also have students reassess their profile over time and compare how their "badge" changes as they acquire new skills and understanding.

- Tools such as SurveyMonkey (www.surveymonkey.com) and Zoomerang (http://info.zoomerang.com) allow you to set up online surveys. You can use the results to track trends and help students see how their self-assessment compares to the larger group.

GET MINDS READY

Good projects start by tapping students' prior knowledge. Many teachers introduce projects with a Know-Wonder-Learn (K-W-L) activity. We describe this activity in more detail later (see pages 100–101), but for those who use it or similar activities, we suggest establishing interest and excitement in other ways before becoming task-oriented with a K-W-L.

This started as *your* project idea, so be intentional in how you instill passion and transfer the project into your students' hands. Start by getting students' attention and giving the idea time to settle in their imaginations. Invite them to open their eyes to the possibilities before digging in. Encourage students to explore and think about the topic, and to discuss their ideas with friends and at the dinner table for several days. This is the ideal time for optimism about the learning ahead. No team has hit a single roadblock; no one has missed a milestone. At the launch of the project, it's all about possibilities.

Imagine this approach to a project: A week before launching a biology and physics project called Colonizing the Planets, a middle school general science teacher brings in a 1970s poster depicting a fantastical settlement on Mars. She tells her students: "People have imagined life on other planets for a long time, and we're going to study what it would really take to colonize planets. You will learn a lot of fundamental things about biology and physics. Next week we have a mystery guest. Up until then, pay attention to ways life on other planets has been imagined over time. We will talk about anything you find."

Each day, just for a few minutes, she brings up the topic again. Excitement builds as students talk about movies, science fiction, and their emerging interests, which range from artificial gravity generators to terraforming (two concepts new even to the teacher!). One student looks on eBay and finds more kitschy posters. He makes a digital slideshow from the photographs, and students debate about what seems plausible and what's just ridiculous. At the end of the week, the mystery guest "arrives" through a Webinar. She is a scientist from NASA's Astrobiology Institute. She describes her work on space habitability, answers questions, and encourages students to inquire as scientists do. She suggests they craft an operational definition of "habitability" and advises how to design research questions. She leaves them dazzled and eager to learn.

The visit by an astrobiologist was really the kickoff of the project. The preceding activities, which took little time or preparation, simply put students in an anticipatory state. By kickoff, they are eager and already thinking, and ready to launch into rich and meaningful inquiry.

Ideas for Generating Interest and Promoting Inquiry

Shake up students' ideas of what they "know." Discrepant events and role-playing predictions are two ways to arouse curiosity and start students thinking about the learning ahead.

Discrepant events are attention-getting, thought-provoking events that purposely challenge students' confidence in what they know. They arouse curiosity and inspire learners to look deeper. An example: A fifth-grade teacher knows her students know a bit about density and buoyancy. She wants to take the learning further with student-designed investigations, so to generate interest she sets up the following discrepant event. She presents two seemingly identical glasses filled with what appears to be water. Over the first, which does hold water, she prepares to drop several ice cubes. She asks the class, "What will happen to the cubes when they drop?" Students expect they will float. She drops the cubes, and indeed, they float. She says to the students: "OK, let's make sure." She holds cubes over the next glass and asks again, "What will the happen to the cubes when they drop?" Again, students confidently state that they will float. The teacher drops the cubes and they sink to the bottom of the glass. Questions abound: What is in the glasses? Are the cubes made of water? What *would* float in that second glass? They design mini-investigations and carry them out on the spot. The next day, the teacher guides students into an in-depth project that has them investigating and constructing Cartesian divers crafted from different materials to operate in different fluids of different depths.

Robert Marzano and colleagues (Marzano, Pickering, and Pollock, 2001) suggest another mind-expanding exercise that challenges students' understanding: a role-playing prediction. Imagine having students just starting a project act out characters (such as Hamlet) or agents (such as red blood cells) that are put in a unique situation, "improv" style. Through role-playing, students operationalize their predictions based on their early understanding of the project's topic. Imagine digitally recording the action, playing it back, and asking students to notice where their characterizations begin to break down (often with hilarious results). What insight or knowledge do they need to be more fluent and accurate in their portrayals? Helping students get in touch with what they know and don't know is a great entrée into a K-W-L activity.

Technology can offer a captivating introduction to a project, as well. Here are two more ideas to get you thinking:

- As she prepares a geography, history, and commerce project called The Silk Road, a fifth-grade teacher finds a set of Silk Road placemarks and illustrations contributed to the Google Earth community by an architecture student in Portugal. To introduce the project, she "flies" students from place to place along the Silk Road. By way of e-mail, they meet the university student, who is studying historical restoration of landmarks along the Silk Road. With a new friend and expert and an emerging interest in the fate of the landmarks, students are ready to begin their learning journey.

- While helping an elementary teacher rethink her tried-and-true shoe-box diorama project of life in the arctic, a library media specialist comes across a student recreation of primatologist Jane Goodall's camp on Flickr, the social networking photo sharing site. See figure 5 for an example.

  She wonders if other student dioramas appear on Flickr, and indeed, a search of the term "diorama" yields 6,012 photographs. Some are not what she wants, but others, she is sure, will give the teacher and her students a fresh view of the

Figure 5 Annotated diorama of Jane Goodall's field camp on Flickr, from Meriwether Lewis Elementary, Portland, Oregon (http://flicker.com/photos/lewiselementary/69461520/in/pool-classrmdisplays/). Reprinted with permission of Tim Lauer, Principal, Meriweather Lewis Elementary School, Portland, Oregon.

project. She encourages students to view a promising set of photos and to write comments back to the submitters. She promises to post photos of their dioramas on Flickr once they meet criteria for quality and creativity. An unanticipated bonus: Students come across Flickr photos of dioramas from *adults* who like making dioramas, as well as photos of full-sized dioramas from the American Museum of Natural History. Students ask to construct a diorama on a larger scale. The teacher finds a docent at the museum to answer students' questions by e-mail. They learn about scaling their display (which requires mathematical calculations) and have new problems to solve: Where can we build our diorama? And how can we design it so people will learn a lot from it?

TEACH THE FUNDAMENTALS FIRST

Before launching a project, think about teaching prerequisite knowledge or skills students need in order to work with a degree of independence in their investigations. High school principal Kay Graham, who teaches a section of ninth-grade science at the School of IDEAS, in Eugene, Oregon, planned a parking lot oil bioremediation project for her students. She knew students would have to know about microbes as a life form and understand their ecological niche in order to investigate microbial actions on motor oil. She taught a series of discrete lessons about microbes before posing the challenge, "What is the best bioremediation strategy for mitigating oil on our school parking lot?" Equipped with a basic understanding of microbes, students planned investigations that ultimately led to recommendations for ridding the pavement of motor oil before it could run off into the water system.

Graham speaks to the practicality of her approach: "By teaching the fundamentals, I was sure my students would be pointed in the right direction when they started the project. Getting to the inquiry stage fast was a goal. I didn't want them to spend time trying to learn something I could teach in a few lessons before we moved on to the interesting, student-driven part, where they started investigating as real scientists do."

Similarly, Georgia teacher Vicki Davis stresses the importance of helping students build their skills gradually before they take on a complicated project that uses cutting-edge technologies. Before she embarked on the global Flat Classroom Project, she had spent a year introducing her students to online collaboration, video production, and other skills. "We had been working with wikis for almost a year before we did this project," she says. "First, I have students within the same class create their own wikis. Second, I have them create a wiki with a partner from the same class. Third, they create wikis with students in another class that I teach." Davis compares learning with 21st-century projects to learning to drive: "First you learn to drive around the block. Then you drive around town. Then you drive to a neighboring area. Then you're ready to drive downtown. You would never put a beginner out on the interstate. You want to build up to that, so they're ready."

Set the Stage for Independent Inquiry

In order to plan for a trip, a traveler needs to know his starting point and have some idea of his destination. So it is with the learning path. When students are aware of what they know and don't know, they can establish a point of departure and a sense of purpose. The K-W-L activity is an exploration that puts students in touch with their prior knowledge and helps them imagine where their learning can go.

In the K-W-L process, students generate everything they **know** on a topic, and also what they **wonder**. This helps them generate what they want to **learn**. If students are already inspired and have had time to think and explore, K-W-L is an incredibly generative and productive activity that leads students into worthy investigations. If done too soon, however, the procedure documents factual knowledge and leads to a less-than-inspired quest for more information of the same type. Also, students often don't know what they don't know, and they don't yet know why they should care!

As students wonder, encourage deeper questioning. Suggest ways to transform factual questions into "why," "should," and "how" questions that will lead to more complex and interesting investigations. So, instead of being satisfied with "How far away is the moon?" help students shape their question into something like, "How did we first figure out how far away the moon is?" Or, instead of settling for "How many bones and muscles are in the human arm?" drive toward, "How do mammalian front legs compare anatomically and functionally?"

Share the Assessment Rubric

Give students the assessment rubric you created for this project. It is their roadmap toward great achievement. Discuss the dimensions of performance (the main learning tasks and underlying skills) and the scale of values for rating performance on each dimension. A good rubric shows students what performance looks like through a qualitative description of each rating. The best rubrics even leave room for unanticipated brilliance!

PREPARE FOR TECHNOLOGY

Technology is not the project, but rather how the project gets done. As preparation for the project, plan efficient ways to get students ready to use technology for learning. Sometimes this will require advance planning. Other times, just-in-time or student-to-student learning is in order.

Refer back to your asset map from Chapter 4 to recall what resources are available to students (such as hardware, software, and technical support). Refer to the Essential Learning Functions of Digital Tools (appendix A) and NETS•S (appendix B). Identify the learning functions (such as bringing people together, deeper learning with primary sources or data, and reflection and iteration) that are important for this project. Ask yourself: *What tools are best for the job?* Imagine these tools in students' hands. *What do students already know how to do? What will they need to know?* Discuss your preliminary selections with colleagues and talk about the learning activities you have in mind to help students reach the "big ideas" you want to reach with this project. A mix of approaches is likely to be in order.

Set Up a Technology Playground

Watch a young person use a new device, say a cell phone or MP3 player. What do they do? Find the "on" button and start figuring it out. Before leaping in to teach about a technology, consider how you might set up opportunities for students to learn by and among themselves. Learning to use a technology or an application for a project can be a rich problem-solving experience in itself, certainly of the 21st-century skill variety. Set up a technology playground where students can explore. Encourage students to teach each other. Watch to see where your help is needed—where a brief demonstration or a more technical lesson may be in order.

At Timber Drive Elementary School in North Carolina, teachers developed a rich heritage project that had students making sense of hidden "artifacts" and landforms at a local park using GPS devices, pedometers, and other tools. Before their trip, students learned to use the technology though a treasure hunt on school grounds. In addition, teachers hosted an evening event for parents, so they, too, could learn. Parents helping with the field trip weren't just chaperones, but teacher-guides as well. An unexpected result was the increase in parent involvement at the school. Many parents had never set foot in the school until they showed up for technology training. Some even took up geocaching as a new family hobby.

Tap Student Expertise

Let technically able students teach others. Set up computer stations, each with one tool students will use in the project, perhaps an online database at one station, presentation software on another, and a shared wiki on another. Do a practice run with student trainers to make sure they can teach important functions. Help them find tutorials and demonstrations they might use. When everyone is ready, have small groups rotate from station to station as the student trainers demonstrate how to use the tools. Make the stations available for a day or two so students can explore and practice. Before students begin work on their projects, discuss the purpose of each tool and set expectations for its use.

Adam Kinory regularly uses audio and video applications to teach humanities at the School of the Future in New York. He says his students have become so familiar with technology outside of school that they naturally turn to one another if they have questions regarding a particular tool or application used in the classroom. "Most of my students have blogs and belong to several social networking sites. These are complex tools in terms of what they allow you to do, but they are also extremely easy to use," he says. Unlike many adults—who Kinory sees hesitating to investigate a tool on their own, or needing to be convinced of an application's value—students just jump in. "Because they are immersed in technology," Kinory points out, "students become familiar with how different services and programs work. The challenge for teachers is figuring out how to build on that. If one student doesn't know how to use a particular application, it's kind of an oddity—but other students are more than happy to help."

Introduce Project-Management Tools

A project log or journal offers another tool to help students track their progress toward goals. A log can be as simple as a checklist where students track tasks they have completed. A project journal can also offer a place for reflection. By encouraging your students to write about their own progress toward goals, you gain an insight into where—and why—they may be struggling or falling behind. This provides just-in-time assessment, and opens the door for conversations about possible course corrections. With practice, students gain new skills for troubleshooting delays or other setbacks. Make sure students understand how to use the log or journal for this important learning function, and dedicate a few minutes at the end of each work period to written reflection.

Demonstrate

If you are comfortable with the tools students will use, demonstrate their use. If you are not familiar, ask the technology specialist, another teacher, or a savvy student to demonstrate so you and your students learn together. Consider asking a technology specialist or skilled student to create a screencast that your students can watch—and watch again, if questions arise later. Again, discuss use of the tools within the context of the project, and make expectations clear.

Technology Focus

Screencasting

A screencast is a digital recording of computer screen output, from either a specific window or the entire desktop, often with audio narration. Most screencasts are tutorials that are created to show and explain steps in a technical process (but imagine other uses, too). The output is generally a video file, which can be easily shared between users through e-mail or on the Web.

THREE REASONS TO SCREENCAST

Tutorials

Repeated teaching of technology skills can eat up time, so create a tutorial once and use it again and again. With a screencast, students can watch the lesson repeatedly from anywhere. Here is a screencast from Web 2.Education on how to set up and use Netvibes: www.edtechservices.com/blog/netvibes/.

Narrated Slideshows

Common slideshow software allows the user to save a slideshow as video along with embedded audio, but the process can be cumbersome. As a substitute, consider turning students' digital slideshows into screencasts accompanied by narration and even music. Then share students' polished presentations with others by publishing them on the Web. The quality of your students' presentations will improve when they know their work is going "in the can" as a screencast.

Feedback on Work Products

Will Richardson has used screencasts to give feedback on student writing. During a screencast, Richardson talks about the essay shown on the screen, and writes helpful suggestions on the "page" with a digital pen. Imagine how writing workshop sessions could develop with teachers and students giving critical and "sticky" feedback through screencasts. View an example of this technique at http://weblogg-ed.com/2005/feedback-via-screencast.

CREATE YOUR OWN

Learn More

See a screencast on screencasting and get advice from experts at the following sites:

- View Steve Burt's Screencast Tutorial at Web 2.Education— www.edtechservices.com/blog/screencast

Read tips from the experts:

- Jon Udell's Screencasting Tips— http://blog.jonudell.net/2007/02/22/screencasting-tips
- Bill Myers' Top 10 Tips for Creating Effective ScreenCasts— www.bmyers.com/public/1107.cfm

Gather Supplies

You will need a computer, a microphone, a quiet space, and screen-recording "screencast" software. Two screencast software products to try:

- IShowU for recording on Macintosh computers (free). http://shinywhitebox.com/home/home.html
- Camtasia Studio Screen Recorder and Video Editor for recording on PCs. www.techsmith.com

Plan

"Storyboard" the content and narration. Look for natural "chapter" breaks where you can break up the material. Watch some effective screencasts and emulate them. Notice the following qualities:

- efficiency—just the right amount of information and slides
- interactivity—the use of illustrative actions (zooming, showing with cursor or digital pen)
- smooth and modulated voice narration
- clarity—no noise interference, no screen clutter

Practice

Practice with and without the microphone. Coordinate script and movements. Consider laying down the screen movements track first, then the audio track.

Record

Follow the advice of tipsters Burt, Udell, and Myers.

Edit

Keep the best and most important information. Shorter is better; three to five minutes is usually sufficient.

Publish

To make your screencast accessible to the most viewers, publish to Flash. If you primarily show a screen capture, publish to .swf format. If the screencast contains video, publish to .flv format. To minimize file size, publish at 10 frames per second (fps) and a simple sound setting at 11.025 mono.

Promote

Add screencasts to your classroom Web page or blog for easy access.

Rely on Your Technology Specialist

Collaborate with your technology specialist to match learning objectives with technologies that help students meet them. Let the specialist coach you so you are ready to help your students. Ask him or her to teach lessons with you. Some schools have students attend computer classes with a specialist, and they can learn new skills in this situation. With advance planning, the technology specialist can provide support during critical times when the project requires special or intensive use of technology tools.

One Size Fits All—or Not

Ask yourself: *Does everyone need to master this tool or application?* If the technology is extremely useful for lifelong learning, the answer is likely "yes." Imagine students mining rich data from an online database of seismic activity in order to assess the risk of tsunamis in different parts of the world. Finding, manipulating, and analyzing data from databases is a useful skill, and the project is a great opportunity for every student to learn it.

Imagine a class using team blogs. Is it important that each student learn to set up and manage a blog? Maybe they only need to know how to navigate and contribute to blogs. The project purpose will dictate how much students need to know, so teach accordingly. If the learning does not require deep expertise but some students are interested, by all means provide them the opportunity to learn. Not only have you honored their interests, you have groomed your future tech support!

Thinking about the usefulness of the technical skill within and beyond the project will help you decide what—and how much—students need to learn.

PROMOTE INQUIRY AND DEEP LEARNING

Guide students as they choose questions, plan investigations, and begin to put their plan into action. For example, a trio of teachers who share sixth-grade students plans an interdisciplinary project on the topic of money. They brainstorm all the ways to combine social studies with science, math, literature, and art in the learning ahead. They decide on the following primary learning outcomes that all students should understand:

- There is a relationship between need and opportunity, and between scarcity and abundance.
- Money, bartering, and other means of exchange have existed throughout history and across civilizations, and they continue to change.
- Modern money has symbolic worth as an exchange medium.
- Economics, health, and well-being are related.
- Money means different things to different people.
- Humans are interdependent.

They start the project by having students wonder for a whole week about a class display: a collection of seemingly unrelated items including amber, an egg, a gong, jade, a kettle, leather, a grass mat, a nail, a toy ox, rice, salt, a thimble, a shell, and yarn. These are the same, the teachers tell the students. What are they? Students ask questions and wonder aloud all week. The teachers ask them, how could you find out? Already, students are talking and asking and researching. Soon they come to understand these items once served as forms of currency. Once the project launches, students engage in a variety of collaborative activities designed by their teachers. During one, teams create their own currencies based on ones they have read about. The entire class decides on a set of goods and services they will associate their currencies with, including a loaf of bread, an hour of babysitting, a bicycle, and a movie ticket. After they establish the value of goods and services in their currencies, teams begin buying and selling from each other, which requires that they establish a rate of exchange.

This complex and engaging project goes in many directions, and while they learn many things together, students are challenged to explore their own interests, too. The teachers are committed to shaping students' interests into real inquiry, so they guide them past the superficial and factual to more meaningful research. A pair of students wants to study the topic *What is money made of?* Their teacher knows this will be a limited exploration, so she guides them to think like scientists. Together, teacher and students arrive at a more challenging question that encompasses the first: *How would you analyze coins to learn what they are made of?* The next question they explore is *How can we find out?*

Consider the limited questions in the left column of Table 1 on the following page. The right column gives examples of how the questions might be improved with guidance from the teacher.

Guide students toward skilled questioning by imagining what practitioners or experts might ask. What would an artist want to know? An economist? A historian? A scientist?

Consider guiding inquiry using question starters such as these, offered by Joyce Valenza (http://joycevalenza.edublogs.org), a teacher-librarian and 21st-century literacy specialist:

- "Which one" questions ask students to collect information and make informed decisions. Instead of asking students to "do a report on Philadelphia," ask students to decide which city in the region is the best place to live. Instead of "Do a report on AIDS," ask students which serious disease most deserves research funding.

- "How" questions ask students to understand problems, to weigh options, perhaps from various points of view, and to propose solutions. Instead of asking students to do a report on pollution, ask them to propose a solution to an environmental

Table 1 Transforming Questions

Questions students might ask	Questions transformed for deeper inquiry
What is money made of?	How would you analyze coins to learn what they are made of? Is the process of making coins and paper the same everywhere?
What is engraving on money?	How has the art and science of engraving changed over time?
How do people make counterfeit money?	What techniques have treasuries used in different parts of the world to foil counterfeiters?
Do any people use gold coins any more?	Is any coin worth its face value? Why is a paper dollar worth a dollar?
How much money is made each year?	What factors influence the annual production of money?
What is the oldest money ever found?	What is money? Why did money come about? What would we do without money?
Whose faces are on bills and coins?	What do the images on money tell us about our culture? About other cultures?
What can a dollar buy in other countries?	What factors influence the value of the dollar? Half the world lives on less than two dollars a day. How is this possible?
How much allowance do kids get in other countries?	What "spending power" do kids have worldwide?

problem in their neighborhood. Ask them how they would invest a windfall of money.

- "What if," or hypothetical, questions ask students to use the knowledge they have to pose a hypothesis and consider options. Ask them: "What if the Romans hadn't invaded the British Isles?" or "What if we paid the same price for car fuel as consumers in Amsterdam?"

- "Should" questions ask students to make moral or practical decisions based on evidence. Ask them, "Should we clone humans?" or "Should we discontinue trade with [name of nation]?"

- "Why" questions ask students to understand cause and effect. "Why" helps us understand relationships; it helps us get to the essence of an issue. Ask students: "Why do people abuse children?" "Why is the mortality rate higher in one developing nation than another?"
(Valenza, 2000)

BUILD TOWARD INFORMATION LITERACY: LESS LOOKING, MORE THINKING

Today's students have access to more information than they can ever possibly use. The validity and utility of what they find varies widely, and two of the most important 21st-century skills we can teach are the critical processes of efficiently accessing information and evaluating its worth.

During the Web 1.0 era, when the Web was basically online publishing, teachers had regular Web sites to consider as sources of information. The Web 2.0 era—in which blogs, wikis, and user-to-user sharable content abound—adds more complexity. The more interactive Web of today calls for not only a discussion of reliability, but also a look at opinion versus fact. What's more, as students become publishers of online content and have the ability to comment on others' work, they take on new roles and responsibilities. These possibilities for working on the Web today create new opportunities for teaching about information literacy.

At early ages, learning to learn from credible electronic resources is an important foundation skill. For young students, narrow the information you expect them to use to a few select sites. Distribute a set of Web addresses or build a WebQuest to limit students' attention to credible sources. Although you may not yet be teaching students how to search and retrieve digital information, you still want to explain the critical thinking and active decisions that went into selecting these sources for them.

As students get a little older, teach them to navigate and search through rich source sites and databases. The American Memory Project (http://memory.loc.gov/ammem), the United Nations Cyber School Bus (www.un.org/cyberschoolbus), and the United States Geological Survey (http://education.usgs.gov) are three of many primary source and rich data sites. EBSCO (http://www.ebsco.com) and other subscription services are other sources of information suited to students of different ages. Start by exploring these sites as a group. Look at organization, examine index pages, discuss search parameters, and read from sites together before expecting independence.

The next stage is to have students search using engines that pull down results they can assuredly use. Here are a few that allow safe and robust searching:

- Ask for Kids (previously Ask Jeeves)—www.askforkids.com
- KidsClick—www.kidsclick.org
- Yahoo! Kids—http://kids.yahoo.com
- netTrekker (subscription)—www.nettrekker.com

At more advanced stages, when you wish students to independently search, retrieve, evaluate, and make meaning from information, consider teaching the "Big6," an entire information literacy problem-solving approach. The Big6 is an information and technology-literacy model, developed by educators Mike Eisenberg and Bob Berkowitz, that teaches about information problem solving for the digital age. The Big6 Web site includes a wide range of resources, including presentations, lesson ideas, a blog, and related readings.

At heart, the Big6 offers learners strategies to help them find, organize, and evaluate information. They become better researchers by applying the Big6 skills: (1) task definition, (2) information-seeking strategies, (3) location and access, (4) use of information, (5) synthesis, and (6) evaluation. These skills are based on a foundation of research into how people find and process information. To learn more, go to www.big6.com.

Your Turn

How to Tell Your Story

How will you share the story of your project with parents, school colleagues, and perhaps a larger community?

As you approach project launch decide which medium best suits your needs. Who is the audience you want to keep informed or engaged? Think about how you could use a class Web site, project blog, online photo archive, video, or screencast "tour" to capture highlights of the project as it unfolds. Would your chosen technology help you manage deadlines? Collaborate with distant colleagues? Keep parents better informed? Encourage reflection? What features would best serve your needs?

If you are short of time or not yet familiar enough with the technology to set up the space you want, consider working with your technology specialist or a parent (or perhaps a student) who has technology skills. He or she can help you design and manage a project space that best meets your needs. At the least, be sure you have a digital camera handy to document your students' activities and track the progress of the project. These images will come in handy later, as raw material to encourage reflection, celebrate student progress and achievement, and communicate about the project to others.

CHAPTER 7

A Guiding Hand—
Keeping a Project Moving

Two teachers were in the middle of an interdisciplinary math and science project that had to do with velocity and different modes of travel. They began class with a question that they expected would lead students to an inquiry experience: *How fast does the average teenager walk?* The teachers had set up a workstation in the school parking lot, complete with stopwatches, chalk, measuring tape, and calculators. They fully expected students to design their own experiments to come up with an answer.

Instead, students began shouting out walking speeds. Paul Curtis, chief academic officer of the New Technology Foundation, happened to be observing. He recalls: "The kids at this school all have access to computers, so they went right to Google. Bam! There was the answer. They saw no need to do an experiment."

That wasn't the response teachers had expected, but they were quick to shift gears. Curtis continues the story: "The teachers pushed back with some additional questions. How reliable were the data? What was the source? How had it been measured? Did this walking speed relate specifically to teenagers?" Students had found more than one answer. That gave teachers the opening to ask an important follow-up question: *How can you be certain which measurement is the most reliable?* After a few minutes of lively conversation about the reliability of data, students wound up out in the parking lot, staging their own experiments and proceeding with the project—at their own rate of understanding.

Keeping a project moving requires teachers to support students on *their* learning journey. It doesn't always unfold the way you expect. This is where the art of teaching comes into play. You need to be able to think on your feet when unexpected situations arise or when students veer off in directions you did not anticipate. As a facilitator of student learning, you want to keep them moving toward important learning goals. That means you need to be curious and observant about what students are understanding and also notice where they are struggling. By remaining flexible, you can adjust your teaching to address student needs. Stay open to the possibility of being surprised—you may be amazed where students go with their projects!

In the middle of project implementation, you may feel as if your attention is being pulled in many directions at once. It can be helpful to focus on how your role as teacher evolves as you move forward with digital-age projects. As you shift away from the role of dispenser-of-information and become a true facilitator of student-driven learning, you need to practice new ways of interacting in the classroom. Students are growing into new roles, too, and they may need help taking on more responsibility for their own learning. This chapter offers strategies to help you make the most of this stage of the project experience. In particular, we focus on areas that can be critical to project success: classroom discussion, technology use, troubleshooting, and conflict management.

MAKE CLASSROOM DISCUSSIONS MORE PRODUCTIVE

What kinds of questions typically get asked in your classroom? Who does the asking?

The teachers described at the beginning of this chapter were reminded of the importance of asking good questions—not simple ones that have obvious or easy-to-find answers, but more complex questions that might generate several correct responses. Good questions are an important ingredient in effective classroom discussions.

Levels of Classroom Discussion

Classroom discussions take place on several levels during project implementation:

- **Teacher to teacher:** The collegial effort that went into project planning continues during the implementation phase. How are you taking advantage of opportunities to work together? Teacher conversations will likely touch on everything from the procedural ("What's our game plan for tomorrow? Who's leading this activity?") to formative assessment ("From what I overheard today, some students are still confused about this key concept. How about planning a mini-lesson?" or, "Take a look at this first draft from a student team. I love the direction they're going. What do you think?"). If you don't have time for face-to-face collaboration, or if your project colleagues are at a distant location, be sure you are making use of a project blog, wiki, or other collaborative tool to keep your teacher-to-teacher conversation going.

- **Student to student:** Students should be talking about their learning experiences as they unfold—within their teams as well as across teams. Remind them that good communication skills are part of effective teamwork and will help keep their team organized and on track. What's more, explaining their thinking gives students opportunities to learn from and challenge each other. In your role as facilitator, spend plenty of time listening to student conversations. Sidle up to a team at work and take on the role of curious bystander. Join in if it makes sense, but be careful not to take over the conversation. Model how to give effective feedback, and then give students opportunities to practice this important skill with their peers.

- **Teacher to student:** In a traditional classroom, the lecture format dominates teacher-to-student interactions. This changes in the project-based classroom. You will still have occasions to talk to the whole class at once, such as when you have an announcement that everyone needs to hear. However, if you are using project management tools—such as a project Web site or blog, an online calendar that tracks milestones, or an online project workspace—you may find you need to spend less time on housekeeping. At times, you may decide to lead a whole-group lesson to introduce a new concept or demonstrate a skill that all students need to understand to move their projects forward. Or, you might decide to use a whole-class discussion to check in on student understanding or wrap up a certain phase of the project with some class reflection. Most often at this stage, however, you are apt to be circulating, observing, and talking with smaller groups of students. This method is ideal for practicing your own listening skills and asking probing questions that push students toward higher-order thinking.

Higher-Order Questions

From observing class discussions and evaluating questions by type, researchers (Cotton, 2001) have found that about 60% of the questions asked by teachers are lower-order questions, calling for recall or recitation of facts. Another 20% are higher-order questions, asking for evaluation or analysis, and 20% are simply procedural.

In the project-based classroom, higher-order questions need to be a regular part of the learning experience—regardless of whether you are talking with an individual student, a small group, or the whole class. Through skillful questioning, you are asking students to analyze, compare, evaluate, and elaborate: *How do you know? What did you notice? Tell me more...* Good questions lead naturally to follow-ups that probe for even deeper understanding: *What do you mean by that? What did you try next? Why do you think that happened? Tell me more...* Such questions require you to be a careful listener—another skill you want to model for students. Once you have started the discussion rolling with good questions, give students time to think before they answer—whether you are talking with them individually or in groups. The average wait time teachers allow after posing a question is one second or less. Yet, students become more engaged and perform better the longer the teacher is willing to wait for an answer (Cotton, 2001).

Of course, teachers should not be the main source of questions. In effective projects, the teacher does not hold a monopoly on information. Well-designed projects should put students in the role of researcher and investigator. Student questions also give you the opportunity to model what it means to *not* have all the answers. You might reply, *I don't know. Whom could we ask to find out?*

Science teacher Michael McDowell explains the critical role of questioning in his project-based classroom: "What I want students to do is come up with questions that will help them construct understanding. They have to go out and explore. At some point, they will hit a wall—they won't know what to do. And they have to work through it. They may be able to work it out in their teams. But sometimes they will come to the teacher and ask. You want to hope you can stay in the type of thinking where you give them more questions to help them get to that next piece of understanding."

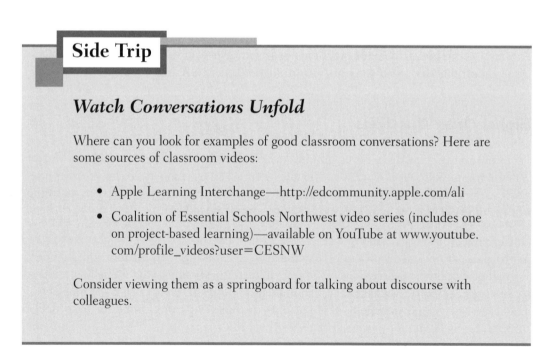

Side Trip

Watch Conversations Unfold

Where can you look for examples of good classroom conversations? Here are some sources of classroom videos:

- Apple Learning Interchange—http://edcommunity.apple.com/ali
- Coalition of Essential Schools Northwest video series (includes one on project-based learning)—available on YouTube at www.youtube.com/profile_videos?user=CESNW

Consider viewing them as a springboard for talking about discourse with colleagues.

Questions for Inquiry

The 21st-century project approach often asks students to take on the role of expert. Team members may be taking on the role of scientist, historian, politician, or journalist. Inquiry is at the heart of many of these disciplines. Students may need help developing strategies to answer their own questions. If students are new to project-based learning, inquiry strategies may feel unfamiliar. Help them learn how to ask good questions. For example, before they interview an outside expert, work with students to develop a good list of possible questions.

An Australian teacher named David Fagg discovered early on that his students had "questions about questions" when he launched a history project, the Australia iHistory Podcast. He asked student teams to do fieldwork to investigate important landmarks in the town of Bendigo and then write and record podcasts that would teach others about local history. Students knew that they not only had the responsibility of teaching their classmates in Australia but that they were also going to exchange podcasts with a middle-school class in the U.S. On his blog about the project, Fagg (2007) explained, "My students tended to want to check every answer with me! This showed that they were not confident in this type of investigation... Students are not used to independent investigative work." He spent more time than he expected coaching them on how to use their curiosity to guide their investigations.

In some projects, students will take on the role of scientist. They need confidence to pose the kinds of questions that scientists ask—even at the risk of failure. The history of science is rich with stories of scientists who worked at a problem for years before making a breakthrough discovery. You want your students to develop the same resiliency to persist in their inquiry, even if their first efforts prove disappointing. If students fail to prove their first hypothesis, for example, your follow-up questions can help them learn from their results, refocus their inquiry, and plan what questions to ask next.

Sometimes, student questions will lead in directions that truly go off-track. Help students remember those wild ideas they wonder about—even if they won't get to them during this project, or even during this school year. The wondering is worth reinforcing. For example, a seventh-grade math teacher keeps a spot on her white board for "wonderful questions awaiting answers." She includes as-yet-unanswered questions posed by students, along with queries still being investigated by famous scientists and mathematicians.

QUESTIONS FOR CHECKING IN

In the middle of a project, student teams are likely to be going in many directions and working at different speeds. That's normal. But it means you need to pay attention to many activities at once. Where should you focus? Think about the kinds of questions that will help you check in on student progress and make necessary adjustments to your project plan. Frame your questions to get at the information you want to discover, and use the right tools to help keep projects moving. Based on the type of information you want, you might ask questions such as the following:

- **Procedural:** *Are we staying on schedule? Do we have the right materials available? When's the best time to schedule a field trip, expert visitor, or other activity?* To track progress toward milestones and deadlines, remind students of the project calendar and monitor students' project logs and checklists.

- **Teamwork:** *How are team members getting along? Is one student carrying too much of the load for the whole team? Are students able to manage conflict themselves, or do they need my help?* Circulate and ask questions to help you assess team dynamics. If you have students using a project blog or journal, ask them to write an entry specifically about their team's progress. Give them a safe place to raise concerns or ask for help if they are experiencing team trouble. For example, consider using an online survey tool or set up a "poll of the day" that asks about team dynamics. If you are using a project wiki, pay attention to who is contributing what to the project workspace. If you see that some students are consistently contributing less than others, use this observation to open dialogue about teamwork.

- **Understanding:** Spend time observing teams at work, listening to student conversations, and asking probing questions. Review online workspaces where you can see student work in progress. If you see students going way off task or basing their decisions on faulty information, ask questions or suggest resources to redirect them. *(Have you thought about...? Have you considered this research?)* Similarly, if you see opportunities for students to go beyond expectations, encourage them to push themselves.

- **Self-assessment:** To find out what students are thinking about the project, ask questions that encourage self-assessment and reflection. Project journals or blogs offer space for students to describe challenges or frustrations, to ask questions that they may not feel comfortable asking in class, or to share their excitement about a project.

Through your use of questions, you may uncover information that you did not expect. For example, the Australia iHistory Podcast project helped David Fagg see the value of aural learning. When Fagg (2007) asked students what they liked about the project, they repeatedly emphasized that listening to student podcasts offered a better way of learning about history. "Even proficient readers raised this as a reason to use podcasts," he pointed out. He probed with more questions: Aren't they also listening when the teacher is talking to them? Why do think listening *in this way* is such a benefit? Students offered a number of compelling reasons, including fewer distractions from other students and the opportunity to go back over the podcast as many times as necessary.

As a result of his observations and questions, Fagg determined that student engagement was high: "They were serious about finishing, and each of them contributed equally to the group." He also observed that students were naturally gravitating to activities that matched their learning styles: "Jackson tended to refocus the group, often asking questions like 'So, what's the question?' David was very conscientious about writing down answers. Clay listened to most of the podcasts, and answered most of the questions that could be answered from the podcasts. They tended to concentrate on the learning modes they were comfortable with: Clay with aural learning, David with written, and Jackson was comfortable across both."

OPTIMIZE TECHNOLOGY

During project planning, you selected the technologies to integrate. When you launched the project, you may have conducted mini-lessons to introduce specific tools, or asked your technology coordinator or media specialist to help your students develop technical fluency. Now, during implementation, it's time to make sure that your technology choices are helping students reach learning goals.

For the Australia iHistory Podcast, for example, David Fagg elected to integrate MP3 players, digital cameras, and a project blog. He had no prior experience himself using digital music devices, but he knew that they were popular with students. Indeed, he was often confiscating them during class! He explains: "iHistory is an experiment in teaching Australian History using podcasts. Currently I own no TV, no mobile phone, and no MP3 player, so how did I come to be doing this project? Part of the answer lies in the fact that I wanted to subvert the use of MP3 players in my classroom. Instead of the endless rigmarole of confiscation, I wanted to integrate them into learning."

During the project, Fagg checked in with students to make sure the technologies were not continuing to pose a distraction. He wanted to ensure they were helping students meet learning goals. Students assured him that the MP3 players were easy to use for making their own audio recordings. What's more, students responded positively to the experience of learning by listening to podcasts. In particular, they liked being able to replay podcasts to match their learning speeds and needs without having to ask the teacher to go back over information they didn't understand the first time. Repeatedly, students told him, "This is a better way of learning."

Sometimes, you may want to ask students to choose which technologies to use. For example, Carmel Crane teaches digital media at New Technology High School. Her students arrive with a wide range of prior experiences in technology. By 10th grade, some are already skilled programmers; others are relative novices. She encourages them to "take it as far as they can go. Some love to create animations. Others are more into programming because of their interest in gaming. Some are really skilled at graphics. A few want to work in video." Rather than limiting students to the use of particular technologies, she lets them follow their interests—as long as they meet learning goals. They then select examples of their best work to add to their digital portfolios, which become the centerpiece of their high school learning experience.

Consideration of the following questions may help you maximize the potential of technology during a project:

- Is technology helping students reach learning goals, or is it leading them on side trips? For example, if students are creating presentations as the end product of their research, are they focusing on communicating key content or getting distracted by creating snazzy graphics? Help them focus on the learning goal.

- Is technology helping students stay organized? Are students taking advantage of available tools to help them organize their research? Collaborate with team members? Keep track of important milestones?

- Are students able to use technology to expand their horizons by connecting to outside experts or a broader community? From e-mail to online collaborative tools, technology offers a wide range of ways to connect students with the broader community. Are students using appropriate tools to extend their reach? Are you using technology to keep parents informed of and involved in student learning?

- Is access equitable? Do students have ready access to the technologies they need? For example, a teacher who uses the workspace and tools from Google appreciates that students can access their workspace anywhere, anytime, from any computer connected to the Internet. And so can she—making it possible for her to promptly answer questions that arise after class or give students timely feedback on their project work. Check in with students to make sure they have adequate access. You may find that you need to schedule more time in the school technology lab, for example, at critical points during the project if students do not have access elsewhere.

With optimum use of technology, you may find students gaining benefits you did not envision at the outset of the project. As an extension of the Australia iHistory Podcast, David Fagg connected online with Eric Langhorst, a middle school teacher in Liberty, Missouri. Their two classes arranged to exchange podcasts, and students became each others' critical reviewers.

As a result, students gained new insights into how to communicate with a culturally diverse audience. Langhorst passed along this helpful feedback to the Australian podcasters: "My students had a hard time understanding some of it because of the speed with which the students were speaking, and the accent was difficult to understand when it was said too fast." (Fagg, 2007) In addition, students critiqued their Australian peers for including background music that was too loud and distracted from the information. The authentic feedback was well-received. As Fagg told his teaching colleague: "The students who did these podcasts agreed with your (students') comments, especially when they listened again to them." (Fagg, 2007)

Technology Focus

Podcasting

Simply put, podcasting is the category of digital media (audio or video files) that are distributed on the Web and played back on mobile devices or personal computers. Unlike "broadcasts," which tend to occur at scheduled times, podcasts are downloaded by the user and listened to or watched whenever the user chooses. With RSS feeds, podcasts can also be downloaded automatically, so that the content is regularly refreshed.

Wildly popular outside school on sites such as Apple iTunes, podcasts can be effectively harnessed for learning, giving students new uses for the computing devices that many already carry everywhere. Imagine your students creating soundscapes, person-on-the-street interviews, or local walking-tour podcasts. Consider how they might respond to a project in which they decide which music would best suit the theme of a certain piece of literature. Or, picture the preparation they would invest, knowing that they are about to interview a local politician or author of a book they are analyzing.

For good examples of podcasting in education, see the iHistory Podcast Project (http://ihistory.wordpress.com) or Julie's Flat Classroom (http://flatclassroom. podomatic.com).

Learn how to produce podcasts with your students with help from Australian teacher David Fagg at the iHistory Podcast Project Web site's "How do I make a podcast?" section (http://ihistory.wordpress.com/podcasts/how-do-i-make-a-podcast). For a thorough overview of how to effectively use podcasting in education, visit *Teach Digital: Curriculum by Wes Fryer* (http://teachdigital. pbwiki.com/podcasting). Fryer also produces weekly podcasts on education. Subscribe at *Moving at the Speed of Creativity* (www.speedofcreativity.org).

Before you begin producing podcasts with students, listen to a variety of podcasts together. Discuss good and bad qualities as you develop criteria for your own high-quality podcasts.

HELP WITH TROUBLESHOOTING

Troubleshooting is a 21st-century skill that distinguishes effective project managers. Help students understand that real-world projects come with real-world challenges. Help them learn from setbacks and fine-tune their strategies for getting a project back on track.

Teacher Michael McDowell says the chance to overcome challenges is a necessary component of project-based learning. "In the traditional classroom, there's no room to fail. It's errorless learning," he says. "Project-based learning is more like real life. You can mess up, but then you have the opportunity to learn from that and make adjustments. There's huge value in that experience."

For example, Georgia educator Anne Davis (2007) was a pioneer in bringing blogs into the elementary classroom. In a project designed to improve student writing, she matched up her fourth- and fifth-graders with high school mentors in another state. At first, her students seemed enthusiastic about writing for an audience. But when it was time for them to publish their writing online, her students froze.

"The room got absolutely still. I could tell that something was amiss," Davis recounts. "I said, minimize your screens. Something's going on. I need you to talk to me." Through questioning, she discovered that her students were intimidated. "They were afraid their writing wasn't going to be good enough for the high school students to want to read," she recalls. What's more, the older students' stories seemed impossibly long. The younger students didn't want to compete. Davis remembers her own reaction: "I was soaring! My students wanted their writing to be *good*. This was the first time they really cared about that." Davis eventually solved the dilemma by talking to Will Richardson, the teacher on the other side of the project. He in turn brainstormed with his students about how to put the younger writers at ease. The high school students went online to offer reassurance, and even constructed some mini-lessons that helped the elementary students break their writing projects into smaller, less-intimidating chunks. That eased the way for the project to continue with success.

Davis emphasizes the importance of conversation as an instructional tool in the project-based classroom. "Classroom discussion has to be a heavy component of this," she explains. "You can't just tell your students, 'Go into the lab and start writing.' You have to build your community of learners, and you have to talk about what's happening while it unfolds."

MANAGE CONFLICT

Teamwork is another 21st-century skill that can make or break a project. During project implementation, pay close attention to team dynamics. If you detect trouble, help students learn to manage their own team conflicts. It's a real-life skill that will serve them well for years to come.

Several high schools that are affiliated with the New Technology Foundation have incorporated the idea of a team contract. At the start of a project, team members agree on their roles and responsibilities and sign a contract spelling out consequences for neglecting them—including being "fired" from the team as a last resort. As Paul Curtis explains, the contract "changes everything" in terms of social dynamics. "Now, there is peer pressure to work for the group. The 'slacker' student is not reinforced by the peer structure," he says. "That's different from traditional settings, where it can be nice to have a slacker in class— they lower the curve and lower expectations. But when students start working in teams, the slacker becomes a real pain for the whole group. The social pressure changes."

By making teamwork a focus of formal assessment, you help to emphasize the importance of this 21st-century skill. Some teachers, for example, ask students to evaluate their peers on a teamwork-scoring rubric. As a less formal assessment, you might ask students to reflect on teamwork in their project journals. At the end of a project, it can be useful to ask students to think about how they might change their choice of teammates in the future. Encourage self-assessment by asking students to describe the skills they have to offer a team.

When projects connect students from different cultures, you may need to pay close attention to how students interact. "Before you start, be sure students understand something about each other's cultures," advises Vicki Davis, whose American high school students have collaborated online with Muslim teens in Bangladesh. "Harmless joking by a teenage boy from the U.S. could be misconstrued by a young Muslim female. You have to emphasize, from the beginning, what it means to be professional."

Your Turn

Analyze Your Classroom Conversations

Teachers are often surprised by the statistics about average wait time or the preponderance of yes-or-no questions asked in most classrooms. One strategy for learning more about your own classroom behavior is to capture it on video and then analyze the evidence.

Ask your technology colleague, a parent volunteer, or a willing colleague to help you make a video recording of a class or a learning activity you want to analyze. This record offers a golden opportunity for collaboration and analysis. Invite your fellow teachers to help you analyze your questioning style, student conversations, or whatever else you are focusing on improving. Then return the favor by helping them analyze their own videos. You might want to look for different kinds of conversations (between teacher and students, or students and students). Think about how you could have taken discussion deeper by waiting longer for responses, asking more probing follow-up questions, or giving students more time to pursue their own conversations with peers.

If you want to take your video a step further, consider making it available for other teachers to use in professional development by turning it into a podcast. Add some introductory commentary to explain your purpose, and upload your podcast to a site such as YouTube.

Section IV

Expanding Your Circle

As the project nears completion, do not overlook opportunities for extended learning. Section IV shows how technology can create new—and even global—connections for your students. Culminating activities make the project even more meaningful by guiding students to synthesize their understanding and reflect on what they have learned and accomplished.

CHAPTER 8

Building Connections and Branching Out

Extending the learning experience beyond the classroom becomes a goal of many 21st-century projects. Digital tools make it easy for students to share their work and exchange ideas with diverse audiences, including family members and peers, local community members, and even the much wider world.

For some projects, integrating technology helps students reach an authentic audience. Knowing that others will be reading, watching, listening, and commenting can be a powerful motivator. Georgia educator Anne Davis (2007) is an advocate of using blogs to improve student writing. As she has watched her elementary students grow into more competent and confident writers, she has tracked a wide range of additional benefits. She sees teacher-facilitated blogs not only as spaces where students and teachers can learn from each other, but also as useful tools for developing student voices. Her students use blogs to connect with content experts, to reflect on their own learning, and to engage in global conversations that would not otherwise take place. "We need to hear these students' voices," Davis says, "and then let them know that we value what they have to say."

Similar benefits seem to accrue regardless of the communication medium. Colorado middle school students, for example, share their sometimes harsh life experiences through video in a digital storytelling project, The Power of Word: Digital Stories (www.davarts.org/art_storiesB.html). Consulting artist Daniel Weinshenker has this to say to visitors to the online project: "Listening to youth is as much a part of the dialogue as giving them the tools to speak. You being here, right now, listening, is vital. For them, knowing someone on the other end is there gives them more reason to shout." (Weinshenker, n.d.)

In addition to connecting students with a real audience, digital-age projects offer almost unlimited opportunities for branching out from the classroom. For instance, your students might decide to consult with experts in the course of researching a particular topic. You may design a project so that your students can communicate with fellow learners—from the next classroom or from halfway around the globe—and become more proficient at working in a culturally diverse world. Sometimes projects generate important information or research that helps communities address an issue or solve a problem, and your students become the experts.

You may have intentionally designed these extensions and connections into your project, but sometimes a project will take off in directions that take you by surprise. Where will your students' learning experiences take them? Now that your project is well underway, this chapter helps you imagine the possibilities and benefits of building even more connections and branching out in new directions.

CONNECTING WITH EXPERTS

When projects are designed to incorporate inquiry, asking questions of experts becomes a natural component of the learning experience.

Sometimes, the teacher makes these connections happen by recognizing a learning opportunity or making introductions online to connect curious students with willing experts. Anne Davis, for instance, arranged for some of her fifth-grade bloggers to interview politicians, academics, and other experts during a face-to-face leadership forum on the University of Georgia campus. In advance of the event, the whole class brainstormed good questions to ask. Student blogs included students' personal responses to the experience, as well as their podcasts and transcripts of the interviews.

Similarly, a ninth-grade biology teacher saw potential benefits for his students when he heard about a deep-sea expedition to be conducted by marine scientists at the University of Delaware. The project allowed students from around the world to come along virtually while marine researchers explored deep-sea vents and conducted underwater experiments. His students even had the opportunity to ask researchers questions in real time during a ship-to-shore conference call that was overheard by thousands of other students from around the world. The chance to ask real scientists about an ongoing expedition propelled his students to dive into their own oceanography research so that they were well-prepared for the conference call. (Information about archived expeditions is available at www.ocean.udel.edu/extreme2004.)

Connecting your students with experts may require some effort on your part. Teachers who make this a regular part of the learning experience often start by developing a list of willing experts. Knowing the skills and areas of expertise of your students' parents is a good place to begin (take another look at the classroom assets survey you conducted in chapter 4). If current parents (or parents from previous years) don't have the expertise you are looking for, they may know someone who does. Use your class Web site or blog to put out the word about areas where you are seeking expert help. Continue to expand and update your list of contacts, using a database or other tool to make the information easily accessible. For example, Robert Pavlica, a teacher who leads an independent student research class for high school students in New York, knows that he can never know all the answers his students may ask in the course of following their curiosity. It becomes the students' task to locate knowledgeable experts. He teaches students how to locate experts online, and communicate with them effectively, as a 21st-century information literacy skill. "I teach students the research process," he says. "Then it's up to them to find the experts and answers they're looking for."

You can facilitate students' experience by helping them prepare for working with experts. They need to understand that experts' time may be limited, which makes it important for students to be efficient at asking questions that get them to the specific information they are seeking. Give students time to practice this skill. Help them make the best use of technology to engage with experts. If they are going to interact via videoconference or Webcam, for example, have students practice using this technology in advance of the actual interview, and together plan an agenda for the meeting so it runs smoothly and efficiently. At the same time, you may also want to develop guidelines to help experts understand what's being asked of them and how to communicate with students.

As you imagine enlisting experts to assist your students, think about how the experience could generate mutual benefits. Kathy Cassidy is a Canadian elementary teacher who connected her first- and second-grade students with preservice educators from a nearby university. Using the comment feature on the elementary students' blogs, university students provided the students with an authentic audience and critical, timely feedback. At the same time, student teachers gained opportunities to improve their own practice of teaching young children to write well. As the project extended over several months, the university participants also got to see the extraordinary progress that young writers can make in a short time. What's more, the experience opened new conversations in the elementary classroom. "Once the university students began commenting and asking questions, my students wanted to talk about the best way to answer a question," Cassidy explained. "They became quite excited that these adult students were reading and responding to their work. They understand that they are helping these 'older kids' become better teachers. The experience helped all of us."

EXPANDING THE LEARNING CIRCLE

What happens when the learning community expands to include not only one classroom or one school, but participants from distant countries and continents?

Jeff Whipple is a technology mentor for teachers involved in a 1:1 laptop initiative in New Brunswick, Canada. He has facilitated several projects that bring students and community members together across distances by exchanging videos, blog entries, and other forms of communication. In one project, a Canadian adventure writer joined two classes (Grades 6–8) for a blog discussion of one of his books. "The neat thing about this project is that the author was real and accessible to students," explained Whipple. "He spent from three to five hours per week responding to their posts. He took time to work with students individually, which got some interesting conversations going." On the last day of the project, the author visited one school in person and read the last chapter aloud. Students from the other school—located a couple hours away on an island in New Brunswick—were able to join and ask their own questions via videoconference.

Buoyed by that success, Whipple was ready to think even more broadly about expanding the learning circle. When a teacher from an international school in South Korea commented on his blog, Whipple seized the opportunity to connect students across even greater distances. The two teachers began communicating about ideas and exploring how a cross-cultural project could meet their instructional goals. They settled on the idea of having student writers and artists collaborate across distances and time zones to create their own illustrated literature—a task that would require communicating in-depth about intent and creativity. Adding more interest to the experience, the teachers imagined having teams of students come together to "judge" the entries, acting as peer reviewers. "It's the beginning of students understanding that there are opportunities and possibilities to work with people who live somewhere else in the world," Whipple explained. "The only barrier is time, not space." That situation may become part of their workday in the near future as they contribute to an increasingly global economy.

The Flat Classroom Project is a notable example of student collaboration across distances. Teachers Julie Lindsay, then working in urban Bangladesh, and Vicki Davis of rural Georgia in the U.S. matched up secondary students in pairs for a discussion of Thomas Friedman's book *The World is Flat*. Using wikis, podcasts, and Skype for real-time conversations, students dug into discussions about the digital divide, e-commerce, and outsourcing of jobs. The project generated buzz within the edublogging community and attracted attention from around the world.

"The international attention took us all by surprise," reports Lindsay. "I think it had a major impact on most students. They knew they had many other people, apart from the two classrooms, looking at their progress. I saw some of them assume more responsibility and take more pride in their work. They all knew there was a real deadline and that they were responsible for working toward that. This was not a project where parents could write letters excusing their son or daughter for being late with homework. This was a real-life workplace scenario, in a way, and the students had to step up to the mark to succeed."

Lindsay and Davis incorporated authentic assessment by asking an international panel of judges—all educators—to evaluate student products in several categories, critiquing the quality of content as well as collaborative effort and use of technology. Adding another layer to the project, the teachers archived the entire learning experience so that other educators can use it to inform their project designs. It's no wonder Vicki Davis refers to 21st-century educators like herself as "teacherpreneurs." She says, "If I have the opportunity in my small school to innovate, then I have the responsibility to share what I learn with others. When teachers who innovate blog about what they are doing, it makes the whole community better." On her Cool Cat Teacher blog, Davis (2006, Nov. 27) describes her vision of where teacher-preneurs are taking education: "Teachers can truly become connectors and breed a new generation of global collaborators and big picture thinkers like we've never seen before."

Technology Focus

Online Collaboration

Many of the projects described in this book make use of online collaboration as a deliberate strategy to extend the learning experience. Take a closer look at the tools that promote collaboration across a distance, and consider how you might use them to expand or extend your project. For a closer look at these tools in action, spend some time exploring the Flat Classroom Project site from all angles (http://flatclassroomproject.wikispaces.com). This project integrated a wide range of technologies—from time zone clocks to podcasts—to help students (and teachers) connect across thousands of miles. It also created an "echo effect," as edubloggers around the world discussed the project. Listen to podcasts about the project here: http://evoca.com/groups/flatclassroomproject.

To help you consider how well various tools align with your goals for collaboration, review Technology Focus: Essential Learning Functions of Digital Tools, the Internet, and Web 2.0 in chapter 3 and examine appendix A for more detailed information.

COMMUNICATING FINDINGS

In some projects, students conduct research or raise awareness to address a real problem. They may harness their 21st-century communication skills to share findings or advocate for change. These authentic experiences share some common goals with service learning, as students learn while contributing to the larger community. However, the project experience remains highly relevant to their lives and often starts with their personal interests and concerns.

Teachers from an urban school in a resource-poor neighborhood of São Paolo, Brazil, collaborated on a project that catapulted students into the role of community leaders. The project began with an interdisciplinary study of neighborhood identity. Students discovered that the polluted stream running alongside their campus—where trash is discarded and homeless people sometimes camp out—once ran with fresh, clean water. They began to imagine what it would be like if Cipoaba Stream could be returned to its previous condition. Students created multimedia presentations to share their research and communicate problem-solving strategies with the city council and local sanitation experts. Their advocacy efforts encouraged others to join the clean-up campaign. Teachers, other school employees, senior citizen groups, and local nonprofit organizations joined the effort to create an urban park to showcase environmental stewardship.

At the Santa Fe Indian School in New Mexico, high school students have a longstanding tradition of using technology as a tool for addressing community concerns. In a project-based class, students work with tribal governments to identify local issues that require analysis or research. They frequently focus on watershed issues of the desert Southwest. Students use GIS and GPS technologies and software to analyze data gathered during fieldwork. While their thinking is higher-order, there is nothing abstract about their efforts. The land they are mapping belongs to their own Pueblo. Students become deeply engaged in working on solutions, as they see how their project will help create a better future. To communicate their findings, they may use 3-D analysis and create layered maps to make their analyses visual. Students often conclude their project work with a video or multimedia presentation to a tribal governing council. In 2006, the school earned a Special Achievement in GIS award from ESRI, joining a winners' circle that included the Library of Congress, OnStar, and many city and county government agencies.

These authentic opportunities for students to share their research or advocate for a cause offer a robust contrast to more traditional "report out" methods at the end of a project—which can seem like an endless parade of PowerPoint presentations. "In more traditional teaching, if you have a cumulative activity, students have a pretty good idea of what you want them to do or say. There's no authenticity or creativity to that," says Michael McDowell of New Technology High School. In more authentic projects, students reach audiences who can benefit from the work they have generated. And, students decide the most appropriate ways to share their findings.

For more examples of student projects with a strong community focus, see Spotlight: EAST Initiative Model.

Spotlight

EAST Initiative Model

For more than a dozen years, students in the Environmental and Spatial Technologies (EAST) Initiative network of schools have been demonstrating the benefits of using technology for a real purpose—to solve problems and make improvements in their communities. Projects make use of geospatial technologies and multimedia tools that are more commonly found in professional laboratories or design studios. EAST students master these sophisticated tools and applications in context while solving community problems that interest them.

For example, EAST students have used GIS, GPS, CAD, and other applications to map the trails of Hot Springs National Park in Arkansas. Using digital media, a middle school and high school team has collaborated to produce an award-winning documentary chronicling a Japanese-American internment camp that had nearly disappeared from their community's collective memory. Yet another team, in a county with the nation's highest number of veterans per capita, recorded oral histories of World War II vets and then used design software to develop architectural plans for a museum in their honor.

"Technology is the hook we use to get kids into significant projects, and to get communities into significantly wanting to support those projects," explains Matt Dozier, national program director for the EAST Initiative.

HISTORY

The EAST Initiative started in rural Arkansas in 1996 and has grown to include more than 260 schools in seven states. It has expanded from a high school program to include students from second grade to post-secondary levels.

Partners from industry and academia have come on board, and government recognition has come from state and federal levels.

Tim Stephenson, who first developed the EAST model at Greenbrier High School, came to teaching after a previous career in law enforcement. "He got the students you would expect—'those kids' that nobody had high expectations of," Dozier relates. Stephenson introduced novel ways to engage learners who were not successful in a traditional school setting. He started with a greenhouse and pond where students raised catfish. Before long, Stephenson was introducing geospatial technologies that had never before been used in education. The first GPS unit was so big that it took two students to hold. Students not only demonstrated that they could learn to use these technologies, but that they could use them to enhance their communities. "All of a sudden, 'those kids' were really coming to school for the first time," recalls Dozier. "They started doing significant things, and people began to notice."

With increased attention came a new question: Was this program the result of an exceptionally gifted teacher, or a model that could be replicated?

A REPLICABLE MODEL

Initially, Stephenson trained teachers who came to learn at his side and took the EAST idea back to their own schools. Before long, the model became more formalized. "We realized we had to provide teachers with significant training and support," said Dozier, a former English teacher who was one of six original trainers recruited to disseminate the EAST model. In 2001, EAST became a nonprofit organization, and today the organization works with public and private partners to achieve its mission.

The EAST model is built on four essential ideas, all of which were part of the original design:

1. Student-driven learning: Students need to be responsible for their own learning.

2. Authentic project-based learning: Students should be engaged in solving real problems in their communities.

3. **Technology as tools:** Students need access to the relevant technologies that professionals use to solve real problems.

4. **Collaboration:** When students collaborate in teams to pursue authentic projects, they accomplish more than any one person can do in isolation.

The other critical component is training and support for teachers. When they join the EAST model, educators take on a new title: facilitator. Their classroom role shifts dramatically when they begin to work with student teams in the technology-rich EAST classroom, typically housed in a self-contained lab. Interdisciplinary learning, teaming, authentic projects, and student-driven learning are new concepts for many educators.

EAST teachers also must learn to let students take the lead when it comes to learning about the technologies they need to understand to accomplish their goals. To support student interests, EAST offers students technical training led by professionals, along with online courses on specific applications.

Professional development is ongoing and delivered in phases by experienced educators in three EAST training facilities. The first phase is a weeklong, collaborative training experience, scheduled during the summer. "It's one-third information, one-third best practice, and one-third inspiration," Dozier says. "Then the kids show up." The second phase happens nine weeks later—once educators begin to run into questions about implementation. "We bring them back together and ask, 'What's working? What's not? What can you do to solve problems? What can you learn from each other?'" At this phase, teachers receive additional training about effective teaming, project management, and project development. The third phase, nine weeks later, has educators explore the real-world issues that their students are encountering. In addition to these formal learning opportunities, teachers receive ongoing support and have opportunities to network with peers.

A highlight of each school year is an annual conference where students showcase their projects, and educators and partners have the opportunity to see firsthand the compelling results of the EAST model.

LET STUDENTS LEAD

As teachers become more comfortable with the project approach, they sometimes find that students are quite capable of leading their own projects—starting with generating a project idea they care about.

Elementary teacher Elise Mueller was reminded of students' potential to chart their own learning path by a student who has dyslexia. Mueller is a regular reader of edublogs. She happened to read a post by Jeff Utecht, a teacher at an international school in Shanghai, China, and author of The Thinking Stick blog (www.thethinkingstick.com). Mueller recalls what happened next: "He wrote about how he hates to write but loves to blog. I forwarded this to Sarah. She said, 'He feels the same way I do!'" Sarah zeroed in on one sentence in particular: "With a learning disability, writing and reading were like kryptonite to me" (Utecht, 2006).

Mueller encouraged Sarah to make a comment on Utecht's blog, and suddenly an international conversation was off and running. Mueller continues: "They went back and forth, sharing strategies for [dealing with] dyslexia. [Utecht] has knowledge about dyslexia that far surpasses what I know. He connected with Sarah in a meaningful way. All of a sudden, the whole world is open for collaboration. It doesn't have to happen at one school or in one community. It can be happening from Shanghai to Bellingham."

But the learning didn't end there. "Sarah decided she wanted to create a resource for other kids like herself, kids who have dyslexia. She wanted to share with them all the strategies she was learning," Mueller says. "So, that's what Sarah is doing now for her project. She's creating a wiki about this topic. That's her writing project. It's her path, and she's tackling an issue she has in her own life. As the teacher, I don't have to be the one who designs one super project for everyone in my class. I can ask my students: What are you passionate about? I don't have to micromanage each project. They can take on their own learning, and I can be there to support them."

EXTENDING THE BENEFITS

If you think about a project having a "lifespan," you might imagine it coming to a natural end once student teams complete their work. Sometimes, however, projects live on into the future to create extended benefits.

In the Montana Heritage Project, students "join the ongoing work of developing and preserving human knowledge." They learn to "think as detectives, journalists, folklorists, scientists, and historians," according to the project Web site. Over the years, students have gathered oral histories on audio and video recordings, analyzed artifacts from the past to better understand current events, published articles in an online journal, and contributed other original scholarship that helps to tell the stories of their communities. Their work is preserved in the Montana Historical Society archives, local museums, and even the Library of Congress so that future historians can build on their research. (www.montanaheritageproject.org)

At Tulalip Elementary School in Washington, a multimedia project is helping to preserve an endangered language. Only a handful of Native speakers remain who are fluent in Lush-tosheed. Students here have created talking books, interactive games, and other Web-based resources that preserve the language and celebrate the literature and culture of the Tulalip tribe. Teacher David Cort sees the Web site not only as a showcase of student work, but also as a resource for obtaining information that is hard to find anywhere else. The Web resources continue to expand as students develop their own technology-rich projects and learn more about their own heritage. (www.msvl.k12.wa.us/elementary/tulalip/home.asp)

When projects have an extended lifespan, they contribute to the culture of the school itself. An Idaho teacher whose students regularly contribute data about weather and water quality that is used by working scientists says students understand that their school is *about* something. Evidence of student projects is visible and accessible, not only within the building, but also online, so that the wider community can benefit from student scholarship.

Your Turn

Where Next?

Think about where you might go next with your project. Would there be value in creating an "echo effect"? Talk with colleagues about the possible benefits for your students if the project were to garner widespread attention. What would be the value of having others know about and connect to their work? Talk with students about how they would feel if their project "reverberated" and took off in bold new directions. What would that mean to them? To prompt your thinking, read the posts that international teacher Clay Burell contributed to his Beyond School blog as he thought about the value of a worldwide student-led project, the Global Cooling Collective. (Find the series of posts at http://burell.blogspot.com/2007/06/green-university-pledge-what-about-k-12.html)

CHAPTER 9

Making Assessment Meaningful

Teachers who use the project approach often notice a shift that takes place when their students begin to see themselves as producers. As Elise Mueller, an elementary teacher in Washington State, explains, "I talk to my kids about this all the time. I tell them they can be consumers or they can be producers. It's better to be a producer. That means you're creating something that brings our learning to the next level. That's the goal—the global goal—with Web 2.0. There's no point in just being a consumer anymore."

Active learning is a hallmark of good projects, and students benefit by being actively involved even at the assessment stage. In a well-designed project, students know why they are taking on a particular task and how it leads them toward important learning goals. They also know what "success" looks like, and they understand the various categories by which their performance will be measured.

Projects open the door for rigorous learning experiences, as students not only master new content but have opportunities to apply what they have learned. Back when you began designing your project, you identified the big ideas—the core concepts and processes—that you hoped to reach. These connect to district or state standards, or perhaps reflect the language of the new NETS•S. When you created rubrics or scoring guides, you made sure that students understood the goals they were aiming for and the criteria for measuring success. Throughout the project, you have used a variety of formative assessment strategies to check in on student understanding and fine-tune your instruction accordingly. End-of-project assessment is the time to look at gains toward learning goals. How well do students' projects demonstrate or apply what they have learned?

Assessing your students' project work requires deliberate strategies to take stock not only of what they have created, but also the teamwork, effort, and creativity that went into the project. A multiple-choice test at the end of the unit doesn't do the job. Instead, you may need to draw on a variety of assessment strategies. The National Center for Research on Evaluation, Standards, and Student Testing (1996) suggests that an assessment system made up of multiple assessments (including criterion-referenced assessments, alternative assessments, and performance assessments) can produce "comprehensive, credible, dependable information."

Your choice of which tool is most appropriate will require you to think about your purpose for assessment. Consider not only what you want to measure, but how will you use assessment to improve student learning.

More than a decade ago, Linda Darling-Hammond (1994) made a case for more authentic assessment: "The way we are going to get powerful teaching and learning is not through national tests. It's through assessments that are developed by local communities, with teachers, parents, and community members involved, so that students are working toward much more challenging standards and teachers are learning how to look at their students differently, how to support their learning better, and how to think differently about standards."

You began considering your assessment strategies much earlier, when you designed your project. You have used a range of formative assessment activities while the project was unfolding. Now that the project is nearing completion, it's time to put your formal assessment plan into practice.

ESTABLISH ANCHORS

Where did your students begin their learning journey? Earlier in the project, when we established readiness, you may have used an activity (such as K-W-L) to find out about your students' prior understanding. Almost certainly, not all students were starting at the same place. Similarly, the distance they travel during a project will not be the same for each learner.

By establishing "anchors," you gain a sense of where students are starting and how far they are going as they work to meet learning goals. For example, Sarah, the student in Elise Mueller's class who set out to create her own wiki resource about dyslexia (described in Chapter 8), offered this astute summary about her learning journey: "My friends write a page in 20 minutes when it takes me about 3 hours."

In a project-based classroom, you expand the opportunities to differentiate instruction and help all learners be successful. In considering assessment, think about the quality of the learning experience. How will you measure the distance each student travels as a learner?

GRADES THAT MATTER

How will you measure student progress toward the specific learning goals you established in the beginning? When you designed your project, you may have developed rubrics to assess progress toward key learning goals. Perhaps you even involved students in developing these tools and helped them understand the criteria by which their work would be evaluated. Now comes the time to put your rubrics to work to generate meaningful feedback for students. (For a good look at project rubrics, see these two developed by teachers for the Flat Classroom Project: http://flatclassroomproject.wikispaces.com/Rubrics#tocRubrics5/.)

Paul Curtis was still a classroom teacher when he began developing his own online grade book. He wanted an assessment tool that would give students feedback across multiple categories for one class. "In the traditional classroom," he explains, "a student turns in a major research paper. If it's late, maybe he's marked down 10 points for each day it's overdue. But the problem is, if it was a B+ paper and now you put a C− in the grade book, you have lost all meaningful data about the skills and abilities of that student. What was he doing well? What does he need to focus to improve? You have not captured that information."

The New Technology Foundation, where Curtis is now the chief academic officer, shares its online grade book with schools across the high school network. It's an outgrowth of the grade book that Curtis developed for his own classroom, and it measures student progress across several categories. "It has become one of our most significant tools that reshapes the way teachers think about assessment," Curtis says. "A teacher might have one category about how well a student knows the content, another about written communication, another for critical thinking, and another for work ethic." Students, parents, and teachers all have access to this assessment data, creating opportunities for meaningful conversations about student achievement.

Even in nontraditional projects, teachers want a reliable way to assess how well students have mastered key content. Jerome Burg, a California high school teacher, decided to give his students a traditional test at the end of a nontraditional literature project. In a study of *Of Mice and Men*, Burg had his English students create a "classics illustrated"–style comic book of the John Steinbeck novel. Burg liked the idea of having students "manipulate" the elements of the novel, just as they might manipulate objects to master a concept in mathematics. In this case, students had to select key quotes and visual symbols to move the story forward. "They have their hands all over the story. That's when literary analysis really happens," Burg explains.

As the project unfolded, Burg listened carefully to student conversations. "They really got at the essentials," he says, "I heard conversations I'd not heard before." To follow up on his formative assessment, Burg decided to do a more formal evaluation of student understanding. He collected typical tests, the kinds published in teaching guides that come with book sets. "I was disappointed," he admits. "A lot of the questions were multiple choice or matching, and only tested whether kids had read the book. There was no assessment of analysis or real reading."

He gave his students a test based on these traditional tools. "I gave the test after teaching the book with very untraditional means, and the lowest score was 89% (and that was from a kid who didn't attend class very often)." Their high performance underscored his sense that students "got it" with this project. "My students had talked through every scene like a director and producer would do," he says. "They knew that story inside and out."

As one more measure of student understanding, Burg showed his students a film treatment of the novel. Again, their response underscored how well they had mastered the content. He explains: "They were indignant in how the film strayed from the book. They were really insightful about the writer's intent, the character's motivation, and more. They had held these characters in their hands. They really knew them."

Technology Focus

Online Grade Books

A variety of Learning Management Systems and Web tools allow teachers to track grades online. Beyond convenience, what are the advantages of maintaining records in this way?

Communication is a key feature of online grade books. With data accessible to students, parents, and teachers, assessment becomes more transparent. For example, online grade books provide a look at "milestone" assignments along the way, increasing awareness of these key assessments. Many high schools that use the small school model, for example, want to ensure that teachers in an academy know how their students are performing across subjects—not only in one class. Online grade books make this information more readily available, opening the door for more informed conversations about student progress.

When grade books are linked to assessment tools, the result is a system that provides students, teachers, and parents with ongoing feedback.

ASK STUDENTS:
WHAT DID YOU LEARN?

Australian teacher David Fagg, who developed the iHistory Podcast Project, videotaped interviews with his students at the end of the project. They were reflective and honest about how the project helped them learn more about history. In fact, they surprised him with some of their insights about their own learning styles. Several of them, for example, explained how they liked being able to replay podcasts as often as they wanted, helping them to review information—without distraction—until they understood it. Many said they preferred this style of learning over asking a question in class.

As an additional assessment piece, students from a U.S. high school provided Fagg's students with feedback about their podcasts. This critical review by peers caught the Australian students' attention and also helped them think about what it means to communicate across cultures. For example, the U.S. reviewers helped their Australian counterparts consider sound quality and speaking speed when producing a podcast for international listeners. They also highlighted the importance of giving a polished performance. Presentations that lacked polish came in for critical review, reminding the podcasters to invest the time needed when putting their work forward for others to share.

CREATE SOMETHING NEW

At the end of a project, you may elect to have students create something new that asks them to summarize or synthesize what they have learned. This novel task gives you the opportunity to look for transfer of knowledge. Can students take what they learned during the project and apply it in a new context?

Educator Anne Davis recalls how she ended a writing project with elementary students who were all English language learners. She had them write and illustrate a book where they used the idioms they had been blogging about. "This meant they had to synthesize all they had learned," she explains. As a culminating activity, publishing their own book also provided them with an enjoyable experience of working together to share what they had learned.

MODEL REAL-WORLD ASSESSMENT

Many projects ask students to apply the skills of professionals in a particular discipline—historians, journalists, scientists, engineers. It makes sense, then, to evaluate students' work using the standards of these disciplines.

Carmel Crane, who teaches digital media, has a circle of friends who work in the graphics and video gaming fields. She draws on these experts to help critique her students' work, giving students the real-world experience of having their portfolios evaluated. "I invite panels in to judge my students' work. It's inspiring for students," Crane says. "The panelists talk about what they do in their careers, and then they give students feedback about their portfolios." She explains that students tend to listen closely to this feedback. "Many of them want to pursue internships in these fields. This is feedback that matters to them."

Similarly, the two teachers who developed the Flat Classroom Project invited a panel of international educators to judge student work. The whole project was a vehicle to promote critical thinking, and this additional level of assessment was a natural connection.

ENTER A CONTEST OR SUBMIT FOR PUBLICATION

Taking the idea of discipline-based assessment a step further, some teachers encourage students to submit their best work to a competition or enter it for publication. These opportunities can be motivating for students who are ready for the challenge of real-world assessment and are willing to meet high-level criteria for excellence.

Science research competitions, for example, may be judged by scientists who apply the exacting standards of their discipline. During the judging process, students may be asked to defend their research or explain the practical application of what they have investigated.

Similarly, writing competitions give young writers critiques from authors who are knowledgeable about their craft. Canadian teacher Robert Griffin has his students submit their news stories to the county newspaper. "If the editor publishes the article," he says, "students receive a $15 stipend from the newspaper, as well as a grade from me for their course."

Your Turn

Review Work Samples

As a collaborative activity, review student work samples together. This will give you an opportunity to talk with colleagues—in person or online—about issues intricately related to instruction. What does quality work look like? What instructional support helps students to produce high-quality work?

As a group, decide in advance where you want to focus your attention. Select several artifacts from a recent project. Have available for reference the scoring criteria (such as a rubric or other tool that describes proficiency). Then, review the samples together, and provide each other with the critical friends' feedback that will improve your practice.

For examples of work-sample discussions and related resources to support this professional development activity, see the Reviewing Students Work Documentation Web materials developed by the Academy for Educational Development at http://scs.aed.org/rsw/rsw.html.

CHAPTER 10

Celebrating and Reflecting

Think ahead to how you will "wrap up" your project. Culminating activities celebrate the journey, reminding learners of where they have been and what they gained along the way. Turn the culmination of a project into a meaningful experience for your students, and take time to reflect, celebrate, and look ahead.

REFLECT ON THE JOURNEY

The pace of school is rapid. Classes barely finish one learning experience before moving on to the next. Taking time to reflect helps students feel good about their accomplishments, but more importantly, reflection can be the thing that makes learning really stick.

In constructivist theory, reflection is acknowledged as being an essential element in learning. When students create their own meaning, it's important that they look at it from all sides while meaning is taking shape, and then view it from a distance, too, as they get ready to step beyond the experience to the next learning challenge. Setting aside time for conscious reflection helps students reveal things they might not otherwise think about: what they learned (and what they enjoyed about learning), their growth as learners, and what (and how) they want to learn in projects ahead.

Remember when you were selecting learning objectives and asked yourself, *What do these all add up to? Why should students care?* Your attention to relevance contributed to the success of your project. At its culmination, offer students a chance to reflect on what they learned and how the project became personally meaningful. Ask, *How was our project important to you?* The answer doesn't have to be terribly profound. If it was an enriching experience that caused students to learn fundamental content better, then that is an excellent outcome. (If it changed their lives—and it's possible—even better!)

Ask students how specific learning behaviors factored into the success of the project. Ask them to reflect on their skill development. If writing was a fundamental part of the project, ask how they changed as writers. Their project skills likely progressed, too. Ask students how their collaborations improved, how they got better at giving and receiving critical feedback, and how they learned to hold themselves and the team to high standards. Did technology skills get a workout during the project? Ask students how they might apply their technical learning, and ask them what else they want to know about related technologies.

The end of the project is also a time to think about growth in learning dispositions. During projects, students experience challenges, frustrations, and joy. Give them an opportunity to reflect on ways they overcame obstacles or persisted when the work was hard. Encourage them to think about how their own creativity came into play to move the project forward. Prompt them to remember when humor and compassion carried them through when spirits lagged. Ask: *How did your expectations of what you could do as learners change? In what ways did you become more persistent or tolerant? Are you more confident to take risks or try new things?*

Finally, help students think about how joyous and gratifying the learning journey can be. Help them recall their positive experiences, the ones that made them confident and caused them to look forward to more. Ask about the parts that are really fun and satisfying: aha moments, weird little things they learned, an unexpected connection with someone, the realization that they are quite good at something or understand something complex. Ask students: *What satisfied you most about this project? What parts of the work really matched your style?* And finally, the *coup de grace: What will you always remember about this project?*

PLAN YOUR REFLECTION QUESTIONS

The previous paragraphs suggested a multitude of questions you might ask to prompt student reflection about the project experience. Having to answer all of them would cause your students to leave the project hating it rather than loving it! Focus on the few things that matter most—those that anchor the learning and get kids thinking about themselves as evolving learners. David Fagg, the Australian iHistory teacher, interviewed students on video to learn what they learned. He had to be a good questioner to elicit meaningful responses. That sometimes meant prompting, probing, asking why, or encouraging them to elaborate.

ELABORATE: WHERE TO NOW?

A successful project is the springboard for the next cycle of learning. As students become more accomplished project-doers, you will put more and more decisions for subsequent projects in their hands. Your project opened students' eyes. Ask students to reflect *and* elaborate. Ask: *What does this get you wondering about next? What do you want to learn now, and how do you want to go about it?*

Elise Mueller, a teacher in Bellingham, Washington, watched a group of fifth-grade boys put their skills to work in an authentic and interest-driven application: they wrote a grant proposal. The boys, who were enthusiastic about multimedia but not satisfied with the technologies available at their school, wanted an equipment upgrade. Mueller relates: "One boy happened to walk by while I was online, looking at a grant opportunity. He heard me say, 'Ooooh!' He came over, looked at the screen, and said, 'That looks cool. Are you going to apply?' I told him I wasn't sure that I had the time. He said, 'Can we do it?' I said, 'Sure! Put a team together.'"

The team used a wiki to organize their grant proposal. They reviewed the NETS•S and other resources, and they designed a proposal for using science and math videos to help younger students better understand the structure of numbers and scientific concepts. Mueller describes all the learning this tied together: "Their work involved reading, writing, and analysis. They built a spreadsheet to track equipment costs. They even calculated what the sales tax would be." And, they had to practice persuasive writing to make their case. Mueller enjoyed seeing students embrace a challenge and employ the skills she'd taught them in personally meaningful ways. She concludes, "This is a great project that I'd never have come up with myself."

Of course, the project also incorporated authentic assessment. The students' proposal was evaluated against applications submitted by educators statewide and had to meet with approval at the district, regional, and state levels. The young grant writers were successful: they brought their school nearly $10,000 in equipment and set the stage for "learning adventures" that the younger students are now eager to pursue. Their ideas range from clay animations featuring "Math Man" to videos that challenge common misconceptions about science. Their proposal also included funding for "dream and share" meetings where teachers will have opportunities to learn from colleagues.

Be sure to ask your learners where they want to go. Their answer might yield a more ambitious project than you would imagine.

BUILD TRADITION AND IDENTITY: "WE ARE THE SCHOOL WHERE KIDS GET TO . . . "

Many schools' identities are tied to their traditions. Is your school known for something special? Some schools are sports powerhouses. From preseason match-ups through increasingly competitive rounds of play, a school and its community rally around the team. In other communities, the school symphony is a source of great pride. Some schools send students to science competitions where they medal year after year. What these schools share is a sense of tradition and an expectation of excellence.

Think about how your class and school can establish a tradition of exemplary project work. Part of the recipe is building awareness in others. When families, the community, and students coming up through the grades know what you are up to, you have a foundation for tradition.

Younger students will be ready for the learning that awaits them in future project-based classrooms. One teacher who left her project classroom after many years was surprised when she met a young woman whose older brothers had been in her class. The young woman said, "I was so disappointed when you left! I learned about the salmon project from my brothers when they were in your class and I attended the class celebration... From kindergarten on I couldn't wait for my turn!" Imagine the readiness of young students who spend years anticipating the time when they get to be part of your class tradition.

As community members begin to notice and value students' accomplishments, they will give you enthusiastic support. After a time, they will expect to be involved. So, invite them in. Ask your community to participate in a celebration of learning. Share with them the challenges and rewards of hard work. Show how your class accomplishments are the result of students' commitment to their own learning. You will make critical friends who will not only expect great things from your students, but will also step up to support you year after year.

The Charles N. Fortes Magnet Academy in Rhode Island has a tradition of doing projects relating to local history. Housed in an old factory, the elementary school has studied ice harvesting, old coins, local Narragansett Indian settlements, waves of immigration that further populated the area, and more. Not content to stop there, the school has become a museum. Student curators build exhibits for the community to learn from and enjoy. The young curators know their work is important to the community and to the students who will attend Fortes Academy in the coming years. They feel honor-bound to uphold the tradition of serving the community in this special way. After they leave, former students visit and take pride in the lasting expression of their learning. They can say, "I made a lasting contribution here."

Imagine laying the groundwork for a tradition of exemplary projects at your school. Once you have established a tradition of excellence, students will feel it's a privilege to honor the tradition with their hard work. As you reach the culmination, think about ways to showcase your project that will establish your identity as a community of learners.

Technology Focus

Photo Sharing

As a project artifact, a good picture can be worth thousands of words. Photographs allow you to capture highlights of a project over time and assemble a visual record of learning experiences. Photos invite students to reflect and think about how far they have traveled. They also help you communicate about your project to those outside your class.

You can make photos even more powerful by using online photo sharing tools to publish your digital album on the Web. These tools make it easy to upload photos, organize them into albums, and add notes, captions, and tags. By inviting others to the site, you have a new opportunity to connect with and engage audiences from your own school community or from all around the world. You can even form photo sharing groups where members contribute pictures on a shared theme.

Photo sharing sites can be integrated with other Web tools, such as blogs and wikis. Tagging photos adds yet more potential for making connections. Tagging allows social groups to form around similarities of interests and points of view. "Folksonomies" (a play on the word "taxonomies") are patterns that emerge from tags, which reveal how the public is making sense of what they find on the Web.

Flickr is a photo sharing site with many social features. Users can set up a free account and post pictures from anywhere via their computers or even their cell phones. Imagine a class sending several student "ambassadors" to a special event. The traveling students document what's going on in photographs taken with their cell phones and then post and share them for their classmates to enjoy as the event transpires.

Spotlight

Starting a "Visual Conversation"

Graduate student and teacher's assistant Linda Hartley from the United Kingdom demonstrates the potential of photo sharing as a tool for learning, collaboration, and research with her blog (http://lmhartley.edublogs.org) and related Flickr site, Classroom Displays. Her site was a finalist for an Edublog Award in 2006. Figure 6 shows a glimpse of this site, which attracts visitors from around the globe.

Hartley (2007) started a Flickr group about classroom displays because she recognized the transitory nature of bulletin boards and wanted to explore their educational value. "They're constantly being created and vanishing," she says. Her project grew into an action research project when Hartley set out to investigate the potential of the Read-Write Web to enhance her own practice. Her blog promotes discussion about the photo displays of school bulletin boards. She explains: "The idea was to widen the conversation beyond the confines of the Classroom Displays Flickr group. The blog looked like the best option with the highest chance of encouraging others to join in."

Hartley had another agenda, as well. "I'd found some evidence in my literature search that suggested that teachers who had had exposure to positive social software and Internet experiences were more likely to use these tools with the children," she explains. "I'd seen the power of blogs and wikis for my own learning during the course of my degree, and I was convinced they were going to be really important for children's learning. It seemed to me that if I could show primary school staff the value of these tools for their own practice, it would be easier for them to see the potential power of the tools for the children's learning."

An online community soon sprang up around her Classroom Displays site. "I'm learning that what I thought could only ever be a community of interest is actually becoming a community of practice," says Hartley. "People are using the group to exchange ideas across geographic boundaries. They share tips, suggestions for improvement, and sometimes argue with the ideas behind displays."

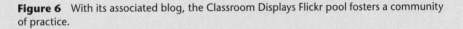

Figure 6 With its associated blog, the Classroom Displays Flickr pool fosters a community of practice.

By early 2007, the number of bulletin board photos had grown to more than 900, submitted by 100 members of the Classroom Displays group. Most images are tagged, which facilitates searching. Hartley explains: "What we are starting to see is a sort of visual conversation. People are borrowing ideas, refining them, and then posting their own version, sometimes with a verbal nod back to the original."

In a recent poll on the blog about the purpose of classroom displays, the most popular answer was, "To give children a sense of pride in their work."

CELEBRATE!

Show student work, put on an event, create a blog, or hold a party. Any way you do it, celebrate learning, and build your school's identity as a place where kids get to learn through projects.

DISPLAY STUDENT WORK

Classroom displays are a common way to share projects with others. What better way to give students a sense of pride in their work? Dioramas, a fully transformed classroom, or a classroom exhibit displayed at the public library are a few ways to show off learning. To get ideas for interesting ways to display student work, view the photographs in the Classroom Displays photo sharing group on Flickr (www.flickr.com/groups/classrmdisplays), and think about how your local displays can "travel" via the Web for others to enjoy.

YEAR-IN-REVIEW RETROSPECTIVE TO CELEBRATE LEARNING

Imagine a year of projects. Maybe not projects all the time, but several of them over the year. When the school year comes to and end, hold a retrospective "Year in Review" event. Show a calendar of the year and remind students of the projects they did month by month. Encourage students to recall their project experiences. Then, assign students the task of each contributing one idea, big or small, that somehow exemplifies the year's experiences. It might be a funny sketch capturing a moment of madness in a project, a dramatic reading of an e-mail from a remote collaborator, a piece of artwork, an accolade from the principal, anything. You documented project work throughout the year, taking photos, collecting artifacts, and more. Make these available to students to work with. Have a wonderful time celebrating your year this way. It's more meaningful than a typical class party and just as joyful—and it's one last chance to anchor memories in students' minds. You will learn a lot right here about what students remember and value, too, which will be useful as you plan for the next year!

Your Turn

Plan a Celebration

A celebration can be big or small, and you will likely scale it to the size, duration, and rigor of the project. But let's think big. Imagine your class accomplished something extraordinary. Have a big celebration! As any event planner can tell you, celebrations are projects! Let students take charge of the event. You might set parameters for the scale of the celebration (no elephants), but otherwise, let students plan the theme, guest list, invitations, decorations, presentations, awards, games, and extras like food, as well as budget for the event.

Make sure any celebration, big or small, includes the following:

- an opportunity to look back one more time
- acknowledgment of how hard work and commitment contributed to the success of the project and a culture of excellence at your school
- appreciation for those who helped (you invited critical friends, yes?)
- a display of the learning, including both student creations (low tech and digital) and presentations
- a look inside the learners with opportunities for them talk about their processes and growth
- an opportunity to showcase projects to colleagues, administrators, parents, and others in your larger learning community

Don't forget, though, that a celebration shouldn't be all seriousness. To ensure that everyone has fun, you could have students create and present their own categories and medals for awards—the sillier the better. Or, try a themed party. For example, if you've just finished a study of an ancient civilization, dress, decorate, and eat accordingly. You could have students write thematic haikus, limericks, or free-verse for a poetry slam, or play a game such as a Brain Bowl, in which students are pitted against parents in a project-related competition that parents are bound to lose. Another idea is to invite a Mystery Guest (even if it's you in disguise).

Section V

Unpacking

Your students may have completed their project work, but your own learning continues. Take time to reflect on what you have gained from this project. Find ways to share your insights with colleagues. Make the most of your project experience by building these insights into your next project design.

CHAPTER 11

Bringing It Home

By the time a successful project comes to an end, you and your students will feel as if you have "been somewhere" together. Like all good journeys, your project should leave you with vivid memories, souvenirs and artifacts you have collected along the way, and plenty of ideas for shaping your next learning adventure.

Good projects don't lead to a dead end. Instead, they open new doors and create connections that you can build into future project designs. When Anne Davis (2007) reflects on her several years of blogging with elementary students, she can see how each distinctive project "clicks and links to the next one." High school teacher Michael McDowell makes a point to build time for student reflection into the end of each project, not only for his students' benefit, but also to help him with future planning. "At end of a project, we do a big reflective piece," he says. "I like to have students identify what we could have done better or what next steps we might take with this project as we move on." Elementary teacher Elise Mueller takes time to talk with her colleagues about the pros and cons of a project. "If something didn't work as we planned, we need to learn from that and move on. That will inform my next project and make it even better," she says.

You invested heavily at the start of your project to structure the learning experience for your students. Now, invest a little more time to reflect on what you have learned, and consider how you might want to share your valuable insights with others.

CAPITALIZE ON YOUR INVESTMENT

Think about the concrete planning that helped to make your project successful. Did you integrate technology in a way that made a significant difference for learners? Have you found new ways to organize your classroom or communicate with parents whom you want to incorporate in future project work? Are there "content-free" elements of your project that you can repurpose to help you meet another instructional goal?

International teacher Julie Lindsay says the Flat Classroom Project has changed her whole approach in the classroom. "It had been evolving before," she allows, "but now I look at what is actually happening within the four walls over the period of time we are contained with a group of students and realize that this is just not enough. Pedagogically, the tools we used in the project I use for all of my classes now. The generic programs we needed—such as for audio recording and publication, file sharing, online publication, synchronous and asynchronous communication, video production, and publication—are essential to extend the walls of the classroom—or flatten them." In particular, she now focuses on the wiki as "a tool that can be the center of all communication and publication."

Lindsay has also gained new insights into her students' changing world. As she explains:

> Fostering student engagement means encouraging them also to think beyond the set class time, to encourage them to continue interaction with project members, and therefore to be thinking about and constructing their own reality at any time of the day. This is how real learning can take place. This type of global and collaborative project opens all eyes to the 24-7 nature of learning. While we were asleep, our partners worked on the wiki and vice versa. This is such good experience for future employment and career realities in a shrinking world.

Vicki Davis says she remembers a point about two weeks into the Flat Classroom Project when

> we saw a transformation. It was like our students grew up. They were still kids, but they became more eloquent. They understood project management, big picture thinking, meeting deadlines, having a global audience, the importance of being professional. It was a tough project, but it was great for their growth and self-confidence. They could go to college tomorrow and hold their own. For my students, this was the opportunity of a lifetime. I know they'll never forget it.

When you think back on your project, recall the most engaging learning activities—the ones that seemed to really "grab" students. Do you see how the activities from one project could be useful in your next project, perhaps with different instructional goals? For example, you might have noticed that your students became particularly engaged in history when they had a chance to examine old documents. You might decide to build an examination of primary sources into subsequent projects.

Did a major theme emerge from the project? For example, was a big idea like "change" fundamental to the project? How might continuing the theme of change play out in your next worthwhile project? Remember, overarching themes help to connect learning from one project to the next.

CRITIQUE YOUR WORK

The project design process may have given you an incentive to begin collaborating with colleagues. Don't let that valuable connection end when the project comes to a close. Plan a "project debrief" with your planning team, and use this opportunity to draw out each other's best ideas for improvement. If you collaborated across distances, continue your dialogue, using whatever communication tools you found useful during the project.

The project debrief is an excellent time for colleagues to review students' work products together. What's the evidence of student understanding? What has the project taught you about how your students think and learn? Anne Davis (2007), for example, explains how her students' blogs provide insight: "[Blogs offer] a window into the minds of my students like none I've ever had before. It's incredible. I can look back through their posts and see how they have progressed over time." Reviewing these artifacts collaboratively offers teachers a rich opportunity for conversation and professional growth.

SHARE YOUR INSIGHTS

As you have learned by now, designing a project requires both time and effort on your part. Don't keep your good thinking to yourself. Find ways to share your project with other teachers—they will learn from you, just as you learned from other project developers when you began this journey.

At the schools that belong to the New Technology network, teachers are encouraged to contribute their project plans to an online database. This project library continues to grow as more and more teachers in the network gain proficiency and experience as curriculum designers. When teachers are planning a new project, they can look to the database for ideas that have been developed and tested by their colleagues and then modify project plans to meet their own instructional goals.

Here are some strategies for sharing your great project ideas:

- Share your project idea with an existing network, such as iEARN or Global SchoolNet, where teachers from around the world turn for inspiration, good ideas, and ongoing projects they can join.

- Create a project library. If your school or district does not have a place to archive project plans, work with your technology coordinator or instructional leader to develop one.

- Turn your project into an archive on the Web. Many teachers create an online archive of past projects, including student work samples and teacher reflection. Flat Classroom teachers Julie Lindsay and Vicki Davis have done this with their project. Anne Davis maintains project links on her blog so that other educators can see examples from previous years. Australia iHistory teacher David Fagg continues to add to his Web site with podcasts and student reflections.

- Publish your project. A variety of Web and print publications invite teachers to share examples of well-conceived projects. This gives you an opportunity to publish your best work, including your reflections about what made the project successful. (For example, consider submitting a project story to ISTE's *Learning & Leading with Technology*.)

BECOME A RESOURCE FOR YOUR COLLEAGUES

Think about how much you have learned in the course of designing and leading a digital-age project. Consider turning your experience into a professional development opportunity for your colleagues, and help them gain new insights into project-based learning.

Canadian teacher Kathy Cassidy, for example, gives workshops for other educators in her region. When she leads professional development sessions, she keeps in mind what it's like to be starting out with projects using digital tools. "I encourage teachers who are new to this to start small. Don't try to take too many steps at once," she advises. "During my first year of using blogs with students, we didn't have any pictures or links. We just wrote. Do what's comfortable, and grow from there." Even as she has become more proficient with using Web 2.0 tools with her young learners, she has not lost sight of her primary goal: "Has this way of learning made a difference over time? That's the goal—and I encourage other teachers to keep that in mind. That's the real reward."

ENTER A CONTEST

Entering your project in a contest gives you a chance to put your best work forward. You may gain more exposure for your project—and for your students—which can help raise the profile of what you are doing in your classroom. You may also get an opportunity to receive critical feedback from colleagues who share your passion for authentic projects.

For example, several of the teachers from around the world who shared project examples for this book were recognized for excellence at the Microsoft Worldwide Innovative

Teachers Forum. This annual event brings together an international collection of teachers who gain an opportunity to learn from each other, expanding opportunities for future collaboration.

Similarly, the Edublog Awards showcase the best efforts of teachers from around the globe who are building rich instructional experiences for their students through the use of blogs, wikis, and podcasts. The awards are based on online voting in several categories, and they set off a firestorm of good conversation within the edublogging community.

ENJOY THE JOURNEY

However you decide to wrap up your project experience, take time to think about how far you have come—and the roads that lie ahead.

"I can't believe the journey that I've taken," says Elise Mueller, who credits collaboration with colleagues as a major force in changing her practice. She continues to grow professionally through both face-to-face conversations with nearby colleagues and online discussions with the global edublogging community. "It has changed my worldview. This kind of dialogue nourishes me as a teacher," she says.

When teacher Michael McDowell reflects on the projects he has developed, he sees an overarching theme connecting them. Since he began teaching with 21st-century projects, he says,

> My rapport with my students has really changed. The kind of questions I ask has changed. The biggest thing for me is that I know my students better now, and I understand their educational needs better. In a more traditional approach, I was not able to address their needs as well. Thinking and doing are two halves of the learning process. In a more traditional classroom, I was doing too much of the thinking for them. Now, they're doing things because they are thinking for themselves.

In her own development as a teacher and project developer, Julie Lindsay (2007) has seen "small steps lead to bigger ones." She encourages those new to the project approach "not to be put off by minor technical difficulties or by critical or complacent colleagues. You and your students, and your relationship with your students, will emerge stronger and better able to cope with the demands of 21st-century learning."

Your Turn

Join the Blogosphere

Throughout this book, you have heard from educators who regularly contribute to—and are inspired by—the edublogging community. If you have not yet joined this interconnected online community, now's the time to start. Use your pilot project as fodder for your own blog. Start developing your personal blogroll of educators whose work you follow. When you see another teacher's post that grabs your interest or sparks a question, make a comment. If you see a project that offers potential for your students, suggest making it a collaborative effort. You never know where in the world the conversation might lead.

APPENDIX A

Essential Learning with Digital Tools, the Internet, and Web 2.0

ESSENTIAL LEARNING FUNCTIONS

Having the functional ability to *make things visible and discussable* or to *foster collaboration* will always be important, even as the tools that help you do these things change. Unlike the tools themselves, such essential learning functions are stable. Once you identify a function you need, sort through a growing array of tools and select the ones that deliver that function in the way that best suits your context.

In this appendix, examine the essential learning functions of digital tools that are useful for any instruction and especially interdisciplinary and project-based learning. Each essential learning function is described, followed by a list of specific tools that deliver that function. The rapidly shifting technology landscape requires that this resource be updated frequently. You can find the latest version of this document on the authors' blog (http://reinventingpbl.blogspot.com).

1. UBIQUITY

Imagine what you and your students could do if you had the opportunity to learn anytime and anywhere. While "ubiquity" is not a learning function per se, it is an overarching and desirable quality of tools that support project learning. Anytime-anywhere access to information, Web-based productivity tools, and multiple communications options are especially suited to project-based learning. When a project breaks through the space and time of school into the larger world, ubiquity becomes something of real value. From handheld devices to Web-based applications, look for tools that help students learn wherever they are, whenever they want, and more frequently, with whomever they want.

Portable Computing Devices

Basic laptop, tablet, and handheld computers let learners tap into their studies and work with others from anywhere. Laptops and tablets are full-functioning computers, but what is a "handheld computer"? Portable digital gadgetry is expanding quickly, and a "handheld" can have an assortment of primary and secondary functions. Mobile phones, GPS, cameras, MP3 players, and wireless capability are combined with small computers, resulting in new devices that make switching from one learning function to another easy. Adding peripherals expands their functionality. Some ideas: Attach a digital recorder to a device with an MP3 (audio) player and conduct "man on the street" interviews or capture soundscapes from nature. Attach probeware to a portable computing device and collect field data to send by e-mail. Send photos or video from a phone directly to a blog to report on an event as it unfolds.

Idea: With your students, make an "asset map" of your portable devices and imagine ways to put them to work.

Learn More: Read technology reviews from Engadget, TechCrunch, and other sites to keep up with new technologies (see the Final Note at the end of this appendix for links and more ideas). Set up a news reader and track reviews from these sites and follow tech mavens like the New York Times' David Pogue (the RSS feed for his blog is available at feed://pogue.blogs.nytimes.com/rss2.xml).

Mobile Phones

Mobile phones are turning into multifunctional gadgets, and even those billed as "just a phone" offer useful learning functions. Most of today's phones let you talk, photograph, do text messaging, and browse the Internet from most anywhere.

Idea: Turn one-to-one calls into class conference calls using the increasingly more powerful speakers in mobile phones.

Wireless Internet

Wi-Fi and WiMax technologies allow users to link their portable computing devices to the Internet at little or no expense. Many public libraries supply free Internet service, and San Francisco, Caracas, Stuttgart, London, Xi'an, Paris, and Singapore are just a few cities that have created wireless hotspot networks or "clouds" for ready access.

Idea: Think about class or team trips ahead. How might ready Internet access be useful for real-time interactions—sending and receiving data, reporting from the field and more?

Web-based Mail and Instant Messaging

Web-based mail allows e-mail access from any networked computer, freeing users from their desktop mail programs. Many young people use Web mail services exclusively and associate their e-mail accounts with instant messaging services. Yahoo! Mail, MSN Hotmail, and Gmail are three Web e-mail services that U.S. students frequently subscribe to. Your students (especially older ones) likely have Web e-mail accounts.

Schools using learning management systems can supply restricted e-mail services for their students. Something else to consider: many Web 2.0 services, including personalized Web pages (Netvibes, Protopages), require authentication, and that usually means accounts are associated with e-mail addresses.

Idea: Talk with your teaching colleagues and technology specialist about school policies about e-mail. Weigh the benefits of using e-mail communication with other options like blogs and wikis. You may decide to create team e-mail accounts for small groups to share in order to consult with experts and register for Web 2.0 applications or personalized Web pages.

Portable Productivity

Learners no longer need to rely on access to computers at home or school in order to create, transfer, store, and share digital information. Two options that make productivity more portable for anywhere-anytime learning include tiny storage devices and Web "office" software.

USB "thumb" drives—small digital storage devices—are inexpensive tools for storing and sharing files. Every class should keep a few on hand for easy file swapping.

Proliferating Web-based applications (drawing, writing, spreadsheet, and even presentation software) allow students to create, collaborate, store, and access digital work products from any Internet-ready computer. Zoho Virtual Office and Google Docs are two of many Web services that provide an applications "suite." The excuse "I forgot it at home" won't mean a thing when students can pluck their schoolwork down from the Web where they created and stored it.

Idea: Set up a collaborative document in Google or Zoho and see how you and a remote partner can work on it at the same time. Imagine ways to use the applications with students and their collaborators.

2. DEEP LEARNING

Most Web sites students go to for information explain, report, or, in the case of blogs, opine. Go beyond "filtered" information where meaning is made by others and help students find and make sense of "raw" information on the Web. Primary sources (e.g., digitized versions of historical documents) and rich databases (e.g., real-time data) are becoming more accessible all the time. Higher-order thinking is engaged when students have to navigate and sort, organize, analyze, and make graphical representations of information in order to learn and express learning. As information piles higher and higher, tools such as spreadsheets and relational databases can help students grapple with what they find.

Primary Sources

Here is an assortment of primary source repositories and archival collections:

- American Memory Project—The U.S. Library of Congress collection has documents, images, film, and more. http://memory.loc.gov/ammem

- America's Story—The U.S. Library of Congress repository for younger learners. www.americasstory.com/cgi-bin/page.cgi

- The National Archives Educators and Students sub-site—Guides students as they conduct research using primary sources. www.archives.gov/education

- Repositories of Primary Sources—Managed by the University of Idaho, U.S. www.uidaho.edu/special-collections/Other.Repositories.html

- World Factbook—An almanac published by the U.S. government, with information about the countries of the world. www.cia.gov/cia/publications/factbook

Real-Time Data

Mining real-time data is possible in the "everything is information" age. The Center for Innovation in Engineering and Science Education (CIESE) compiled more than 100 real-time data sources at www.k12science.org/realtimedatasites.html. Here are a few examples from the site to help you imagine the possibilities:

- Radio Meteors—Listen and track meteors as they enter the earth's atmosphere.

- Oceanweather.inc—Collect real-time weather data from ships and buoys.

- Morbidity and Mortality Weekly Report—Use up-to-the-minute data to chart health trends.

- WhaleNet Active Satellite Tags—Use satellite monitoring data to track whale migration.

Other real-time data sets are available from these sources:

- Worldometers—Tickers continuously update world population data, carbon emissions, hunger, deforestation, and more. www.worldometers.info

- U.S. Geological Survey—Real-time data on water and earthquakes with geospatial databases. www.usgs.gov

- Numbers in Search of a Problem from Schools of California Online Resources for Education (SCORE) Mathematics—Study sports statistics, stock quotes, lending rates, and more. http://score.kings.k12.ca.us/junkdrawer.html

Students can contribute to data sets, too. For example, on the Global Grocery List Project site (http://landmark-project.com/ggl), students around the world share local grocery prices to build a growing table of data.

Web-based Tools for Making Sense of Data

Learners can interpret and make visual displays of the data they mine or collect with Web-based tools such as spreadsheets, relational databases, and chart and graph creators. Examples include the following:

- Google Docs—This Web-based application allows users to upload or create spreadsheets and share, manage, and manipulate data online. http://docs.google.com

- Zoho Virtual Office—This Web-based productivity suite is one of several that offer spreadsheets. www.zoho.com

- These three sites offer database tools to manage, share, and explore data:

  o Dabble DB—http://www.dabbledb.com

  o Lazybase—http://lazybase.com

  o Zoho Creator—http://creator.zoho.com

- Create a Graph—This Web-based graph creator is at Kid Zone, a sub-site of the National Center for Education Statistics site. http://nces.ed.gov/nceskids/createagraph

3. MAKING THINGS VISIBLE AND DISCUSS-ABLE

There are many good reasons to "make things visible" with digital tools: showing rather than telling; understanding where (and who) we are in relation to others; conceptualizing with mind maps; seeing things too big or too small or too fast or too slow for the naked eye; watching events unfold; examining history through digital artifacts; expressing ideas through photography, multimedia, and digital art; and conceptualizing with graphical representations, modeling, and animation. A picture is worth a thousand words, and making thoughts and ideas visible and sharable is the first step in getting the conversation going.

Maps and More

Take in a Worldview

Google Earth makes the world visible and understandable in too many ways to mention. The best way to understand Google Earth is to experience it. "Fly" from your house to Paris. Examine placemarks along the "Silk Road." See how communities of users share location-specific information with photos and data feeds. Read the chapter 2 Spotlight about Google Lit Trips (www.googlelittrips.org) for inspiration.

Idea: Learn how Google Earth "mashups" combine the power of Google Earth with real-time information services. Visit the Google Earth information page at Google for Educators: http://www.google.com/educators/p_earth.html.

Where are We?

Web-based mapping services tap into huge databases to supply precise maps, directions, and landmark tags or placemarks. Improve students' spatial relations and knowledge of geography using interactive maps such as the following:

- Yahoo! Maps—http://maps.yahoo.com

- MapQuest—www.mapquest.com

- Google Maps—http://maps.google.com

Idea: Learn how mashups combine the power of maps with real-time information services. Some mashups to get you started:

- Public 911—Incoming 911 emergency calls in a growing list of cities, displayed on a continually refreshing Google map. www.public911.com

- Shakespeare Explorer—Synchronized Yahoo map and time line about the life and legacy of William Shakespeare. www.kennedy-center.org/explorer/shakespeare

Idea: Follow the UK blog Digital Geography (www.digitalgeography.co.uk), which tracks how new technologies are used to learn about everything from tectonics to wind farms.

Words into Visual Arrays

The Thinkmap Visual Thesaurus (www.visualthesaurus.com) is an interactive dictionary and thesaurus with an innovative display that encourages exploration, learning, and word play. Relational word webs capture the nuances of language in ways regular reference books cannot. After five free lookups, the Visual Thesaurus requires a subscription at a nominal fee.

Idea: As you play with the Visual Thesaurus, imagine the power of projecting these interactive webs whenever your class wonders about a word. See how a simple inquiry turns into a rich and wonderful exploration.

Webcams

As the story goes, the first Web camera was trained on a coffee pot, saving the innovator the trouble of traveling down several flights of stairs to the staff room only to find an empty pot. Use Webcams to view extreme weather, the panorama from the Eiffel Tower, and many zoo exhibits. The site EarthCam tracks thousands of Webcams. Stay within their Education domain (http://search.earthcam.com/search/adv_search.php?cat[]=EDU) to avoid questionable content.

Idea: Imagine the possibilities for using Webcam imagery as you read about UK extreme geographer Tony Cassidy's "Web-cam Wall," in which Cassidy flows multiple camera feeds into a single PowerPoint slide for a captivating effect. http://pilotgcseradicalgeography .co.uk/2007/04/02/web-cam-wall

Mind Mapping

Move beyond classic desktop mind mapping software and try Web-based applications that allow simultaneous contributions by remote users. Here are a few to try:

- Mindomo—www.mindomo.com
- bubbl.us—www.bubbl.us
- Kayuda—www.kayuda.com
- MindMeister—www.mindmeister.com

Photographs Online

Flickr (http://www.flickr.com) and Picasa (http://picasa.google.com) are two photo shar-ing Web services that are easy and fun to use. Picasa syncs up nicely with a Google personalized home page and is adding community features all the time. Flickr (which, along with del.icio.us, put the social "folksonomy" concept on the map) has tagging and sorting functions that encourage collaboration and build community among like-minded users. Many images on Flickr are submitted to the "creative commons" and can be used royalty-free. Search for photographs you can teach with ("diorama" returns 7,302 images), and post students' photographs into collections to share with others. Consider adding a Flickr feed to illustrate your class blog. See how Meriwether Lewis Elementary School in Portland, Oregon, uses a Flickr feed to show fresh photos on the school's site, http:// lewiselementary.org.

Idea: Join a Flickr group such as Classroom Displays (www.flickr.com/groups/ classrmdisplays) to see how collaboration happens with this medium. Browse the photos and meet group members who are interested in what we show in our classrooms.

Virtual Manipulatives and Modeling Software

Here are sites and resources that use the power of the Web to help students with patterns, data analysis, probability, geometry, physics, chemistry and even architecture:

- National Library of Virtual Manipulatives—Sponsored by the National Science Foundation. http://nlvm.usu.edu/en/nav/vlibrary.html
- Illuminations—The National Council of Teachers of Mathematics hosts interactive applets and associated lessons through this portal. http://illuminations .nctm.org
- Google SketchUp—Developed for working through the conceptual stages of design, this software allows students to create 3-D models. Add SketchUp "buildings" to your Google maps. See the SketchUp page on Google Educator to get started. www.google.com/educators/p_sketchup.html

Concept Modeling

Intel Corporation offers a set of interactive reasoning tools that help students rate and rank, grapple with forces in systems, and construct a well-reasoned argument. See Visual Ranking, Seeing Reason, and Showing Evidence tools and associated curriculum at www.intel.com/education/tools/.

4. EXPRESSING OURSELVES, SHARING IDEAS, BUILDING COMMUNITY

The World Wide Web has evolved from an information medium into a social medium, and opportunities for expression continue to grow. Students using MySpace and instant messaging are accustomed to these forms of personal interaction. Imagine the parallels in school and ways students can use the Web to express their ideas and build society around shared interests. Connect your class to the world using a Web site, blog, wiki, or a virtual world like Second Life. Have students "tag" Web content and share tags with others. (You will be surprised how social connections form just by sharing tags.)

Web Sites and Blogs and Hybrids

Bottom line, your class will want to have a digital face for the world when you are in project mode. The division between blogs and Web pages is blurring a bit as content management becomes more fluid. The kind of site you build will depend on the functions you want.

Regular Web Sites

Your district may support class Web pages associated with the school site. This may be a first step in transmitting information to the bigger world, but static sites don't offer the function of two-way communication like blogs and dynamic Web sites can. If this is how you choose to start letting others know about your projects, be sure to advise families and community members to check in regularly, or notify them by e-mail when you update the site.

If the district does not support class pages, consider trying a free Web hosting service. Below are two that don't have banner or pop-up ads (the usual cost of "free" services). Again, let your wider community know when you update.

- Google Page Creator—Online tool for anyone to create and publish simple web pages. www.pages.google.com

- Doteasy—Free hosting without ad banners. Includes e-mail addresses, unlimited FTP access, and more. www.doteasy.com

If you want to present many kinds of media, such as streaming video, news feeds, podcasts, or downloadable files, and if you want participation by readers, create a dynamic Web site or blog. Here is more information on these blurring environments:

More Web than blog: Check out hosting services that let you build a Web site with advanced functionality, such as Site 5 and Dreamhost. These offer multiple services beyond hosting and site administration controls for your Web pages, including a blog auto installer, e-mail accounts, 15 GB of Web storage, Web mail, and more. Services such as these cost around $10.00 per month.

More blog than Web: You can create Web pages along with your blog. Wordpress is one popular and free blog service that does this. Although Wordpress is free, it requires a compatible hosting environment, which will cost between $6.00 and $8.00 a month. Wordpress recommends BlueHost, AN Hosting, Yahoo! Web Hosting, Dream Host, and Laughing Squid.

Beyond the Newsletter: Blogs for Expression and Reporting

Note: For blogs as a reflection tool, see 8. Reflection and Iteration, in this appendix. Blogging tools are discussed there as well.

For the purposes of expression, think of a blog as a simple web page that an individual or group uses to present their ideas. A student might keep a journal in a blog to share her thoughts. A class might maintain a blog in order to show parents and others what is going on in a project. A blog allows visitors to comment on any article, or "post," they read, which is a nice way for students to hear from the outside world. Imagine a class blog with posts as well as syndicated "feeds," or information that flows from sources such as a photo site, a school calendar, a news outlet, or even a dictionary word-of-the-day. Syndicate your class blog so everyone who reads it knows whenever something new has been posted.

Idea: Start reading blogs to see how they differ from more static Web pages. Look at A Duck with a Blog (http://duckdiaries.edublogs.org), a simple class blog where young students published on a single topic over several months. Notice the ClustrMap showing visits to the blog from around the world.

Blogs for Building Community

The society-building part of blogging begins when bloggers loosely connect around a shared topic of interest. The prolific members of the edublogger community—see a short list of edublogs in chapter 1—are up-to-date, provocative writers who share their thoughts on education and offer dispatches from the field. They report and opine about education technologies, conference proceedings, their own workshops, and interactions with educators and kids. Bloggers often publish a "blogroll," a set of links to other bloggers with whom they feel kinship.

Idea: Read a blog on a topic of interest and see how that author connects you to other bloggers. Blogs are bountiful sources of information. As you read awhile, you will settle in with those bloggers whose expertise and authority you trust.

Get Started

A class blog will serve you in myriad ways and can be easier to maintain than more complex, dynamic Web sites. To begin, explore the functions of a free blog like those hosted by Edublog, Blogger, or Blogmeister. If you want more design options and administrative controls, try Wordpress, which is also free. With your free blog, you can publish news like you would in a paper newsletter and add pictures easily. But, unlike the newsletter, a blog invites participation. When visitors come to the site they can write comments about the posts they read, and even comment on comments. You can send automated e-mail updates to everyone interested in your class blog whenever you change material on the site. To do this, set up FeedBurner, which recognizes when new content is added to your site and pushes it out to subscribers as e-mail. FeedBurner works behind the scenes, taking care of list management and verification and responding whenever new content is available to send. Since FeedBurner sends out an update as e-mail, recipients are likely to reply to you in e-mail, too—just another way your blog can invite interaction. To see an example of a school site that uses FeedBurner, see Sellwood (Oregon) Middle School's site, www.sellwoodmiddleschool.org/alpha. Look for "Subscribe to Sellwood News" to get the idea.

5. COLLABORATION— TEACHING AND LEARNING WITH OTHERS

Projects invite collaboration. Tools abound that help us learn together. Use exchange services to find experts or fellow learners. Use shared Web applications to plan and write together. Plan virtual experiences that allow people to "meet." Use survey tools to take the pulse of the community. Examples include the following: wikis, Google Docs, podcasts and webinars, and survey tools.

Engage Experts

Chapter 4 has readers create an asset map—a visual display of all the talent, tools, spaces, and support that can be put to use in project learning. As you seek expertise, look back at your asset map and think about experts in your own community whom you might engage. Think of ways to interact with them both in person and using e-mail, a wiki, or other digital tools. Once you've exhausted local resources, turn to remote experts for help. The nearest university may be the place to start, or consider one of these clearinghouses:

- The Virtual Reference Desk AskA Service—This service from the Digital Reference Education Initiative introduces students to research librarians who are experts on topics from architecture to zoology. http://vrd.askvrd.org/

- The Electronic Emissary—Hosted by the School of Education at the College of William and Mary, this site helps kindergarten through Grade 12 teachers and students locate mentors who are experts in various disciplines. http://emissary.wm.edu

Engage Other Learners

Think about your project. Who would be interested in studying with you? A school nearby, older adults, college students, a classroom across the world? Imagine who shares interest in your topic and engage them. To find remote collaborators, visit project clearinghouses to connect your students with other learners studying the same topic. Note: Find a variety of project sites in chapter 2.

If a project idea hasn't emerged yet, set up a simple e-mail exchange and see where it goes. The Intercultural E-mail Classroom Connections (IECC; http://www.iecc.org) service is a good place to start an e-mail exchange. Since 1992, IECC has helped teachers around the globe arrange intercultural e-mail connections among their students. A new service, IECC-INTERGEN, helps teachers and their classrooms create intergenerational partnerships with volunteers who are over 50 years of age.

Hold Virtual Meetings

Use virtual meeting software to host meetings with anyone in the world. Virtual meeting brokers allow remote participants to interact and even take turns controlling the meeting. Services can include screen sharing, whiteboards, chat, and more. Test out the following virtual meeting services for free before subscribing:

- WebEx—www.webex.com
- Adobe Acrobat Connect—http://onlineservices.adobe.com
- GoToMeeting—www.gotomeeting.com

Connect through Webinars

A Webinar is a Web-based seminar with video. Imagine having an expert "visit" your class via computer projection. With a Webinar service, computer video camera, and microphone, a presenter and audience can interact as if they are in the same room.

Test out these Webinar services for free before subscribing:

- GoToWebinar—www.gotowebinar.com
- WebEx—www.webex.com

Talk over the Computer

It is now possible to speak to others through your computer as you would over the phone. Voice-over internet protocol (voice-over IP) services such as Skype and Gizmo let you call from your computer to another computer or to a telephone anywhere in the world. Not only do they support voice, but many services offer instant messaging and video. You are not limited to two-way communication—host a conference call of any reasonable size with Skype or the other services. Imagine your students going home and saying: "I talked with my collaborators in Singapore and Tokyo today."

- Skype—To talk with others using your computers, you all need to have is Skype. No set up is necessary for calling ordinary phones. www.skype.com

- Gizmo—Gizmo offers free calling to any Gizmo Project, Yahoo! Messenger, Google Talk, or Windows Live user. www.gizmoproject.com

Collaborate

Wikis

A wiki is a great tool for planning and writing together. Organize the site to match the structure of your project, then invite others to write with you. Wikis are rarely the place to publish a final draft. Think of the wiki as the "workroom," and a blog or Web page as the "showroom." See more on wikis in section 8 Reflection and Iteration in this appendix.

Web-based Applications

Collaborate on a Web-based product (such as a document, spreadsheet, or presentation) using applications such as Google Docs or ZohoCreator.

6. RESEARCH

Projects invariably involve research, and for most research questions students turn directly to the Web. Internet research puts information literacy to the test. Quality directories, search engines with filtering, a variety of bookmark tagging tools, and citation "engines" help students make sense of and organize what they need from the ever-expanding Web.

Quality Directories

- Ask for Kids—Designed for K–12 learners, Ask offers a search engine plus study help with an almanac, biography index, dictionary, and thesaurus; math, science, and astronomy information; clip art; and more. www.askforkids.com

- Infoplease—This site offers many "desk reference" tools. www.infoplease.com

- International Children's Digital Library—This collection that represents outstanding historical and contemporary books from around the world. www.icdlbooks.org

Kid Search Engines

- AOL@School—A search engine and directory with sites selected by online education experts. www.aolatschool.com/students

- KidsClick!—A Web search for kids by librarians. www.kidsclick.org

Safe Search

- AltaVista Family Filter—The Family Filter option is available from the settings page and may be protected with a password. www.altavista.com

- Google SafeSearch—Go to the preferences section to turn on filtering. www.google.com

- Lycos Adult Content Filter—Go to the Advanced Search section to set the adult content filter. www.lycos.com

- Yahoo SafeSearch—Select preferred SafeSearch setting in Advanced Search. www.yahoo.com

Bookmarks and Citations

Bookmarking tools help users organize Web sources and share ideas about what they find with others. The social bookmarking site del.icio.us (http://del.icio.us) allows storing and sharing of web bookmarks. Note: Find more about bookmarking in chapter 1 Technology Focus: Social Bookmarking.

The Citation Machine (http://citationmachine.net), from David Warlick's Landmarks Project, makes teaching students proper acknowledgement of references easy. Not just for books, the engine formats citations for Web sources, newspapers, and other common references.

7. PROJECT MANAGEMENT

During projects, students need to manage time, work, sources, feedback from others, drafts, and products. A simple folder on the district server or a workspace in the school's Learning Management System may suffice, but consider Web-based "home pages" or "desktops" that give students a space to work and associated tools (calendars, to-do lists) to help them plan and organize. They can get to their home page from anywhere at any time. Personalized desktops are changing rapidly. See a few in action before selecting the ones to use with students. Examples include the following:

- iGoogle—www.google.com/ig
- My Yahoo!—http://my.yahoo.com
- Netvibes—www.netvibes.com
- Pageflakes—www.pageflakes.com
- Protopage—www.protopage.com

Idea: Set up your own environment, and use it for a while to discover ways to use personalized Web pages with your students.

Learn More: For a screencast tutorial on creating a Web homepage in Netvibes, see Web 2.Education at www.edtechservices.com/blog/netvibes/.

8. REFLECTION AND ITERATION

Deep learning happens when you examine your ideas from all sides and from other points of view. Reconsidering and reshaping ideas to bring them to high polish is the difference between passable and masterful work. Blogs and wikis give learners the opportunity to shape their work and expose it to the critical feedback of others.

Blogs

A blog can serve as a personal diary or journal, where students put their thinking out on the table to give it a good look and elicit alternative perspectives. The David Warlick site ClassBlogmeister (http://classblogmeister.com) outlines a writing process using blogs that promotes cycles of drafting, feedback, and revision.

Blog entries spanning the life of a project let others watch how learning takes shape and, at the end, can serve as lasting artifacts of the learning process.

Blog-hosting sites particularly suited for school:

- Edublogs—Free blogs for teachers, students, and English language learners, supported by WordPress. http://edublogs.org

- Blogmeister—Free blogs for teachers and students from David Warlick and the Landmark Project. Great advice here on how to use blogs to shape writing. http://classblogmeister.com

Other free blog services are listed below, and some are very easy to use. Be careful of features that let student or family readers go to a random "next blog," or allow spam content to populate comments boxes.

- Blogger—www.blogger.com

- LiveJournal—www.livejournal.com

- Windows Live Spaces—http://home.services.spaces.live.com

- Moveable Type—www.sixapart.com/moveabletype

- WordPress—http://wordpress.com

Idea: Go to blog host Blogmeister (http://classblogmeister.com) to see a variety of classroom blogs from around the United States.

Wikis

Wikis are useful for drafting iterations of work and sharing works in progress. Using version histories, a writer can look back at (and even retrieve) earlier drafts. Any number of people can collaborate on a wiki. Imagine the possibilities for sharing, writing, and editing together using a wiki.

Some wikis are public. For school projects, use administrator controls to limit access to those involved in a class project.

- MediaWiki—(engine for Wikipedia) www.mediawiki.org

- PBWiki—http://pbwiki.com

- Wikispaces—www.wikispaces.com

If you are not ready to go "live" with a wiki, try Instiki. The program runs on a classroom computer and can provide a wiki environment from within a classroom. Learn more from the *eSchool News* article at www.eschoolnews.com/eti/2004/10/000172.php.

Idea: If you have never visited Wikipedia, go to www.wikipedia.org and see what happens when people collectively attempt to explain the world. In early 2007, Wikipedia displayed 1,688,000 encyclopedia entries in English alone.

Idea: Find other teachers who are using wikis and see what is happening in these learning spaces. One to visit: Paul Allison's High School Online Collaborative Writing wiki (http://schools.wikia.com/wiki/Main_Page).

Final Note

For a one-stop discussion of Web-based applications, examine the Office 2.0 Database at http://o20db.com. For a deeper dive into all things technical, try TechCrunch (www.techcrunch.com), Gizmodo (http://www.gizmodo.com), and Engadget (www.engadget.com). And for fun that spills from technology over into life, try Lifehacker (http://lifehacker.com).

APPENDIX B

National Educational Technology Standards for Students (NETS•S)

1. CREATIVITY AND INNOVATION

Students demonstrate creative thinking, construct knowledge, and develop innovative products and processes using technology. Students:

   a.   apply existing knowledge to generate new ideas, products, or processes.

   b.   create original works as a means of personal or group expression.

   c.   use models and simulations to explore complex systems and issues.

   d.   identify trends and forecast possibilities.

2. COMMUNICATION AND COLLABORATION

Students use digital media and environments to communicate and work collaboratively, including at a distance, to support individual learning and contribute to the learning of others. Students:

   a.   interact, collaborate, and publish with peers, experts or others employing a variety of digital environments and media.

   b.   communicate information and ideas effectively to multiple audiences using a variety of media and formats.

   d.   develop cultural understanding and global awareness by engaging with learners of other cultures.

   d.   contribute to project teams to produce original works or solve problems.

3. RESEARCH AND INFORMATION FLUENCY

Students apply digital tools to gather, evaluate, and use information. Students:

  a. plan strategies to guide inquiry.

  b. locate, organize, analyze, evaluate, synthesize, and ethically use information from a variety of sources and media.

  c. evaluate and select information sources and digital tools based on the appropriateness to specific tasks.

  d. process data and report results.

4. CRITICAL THINKING, PROBLEM SOLVING AND DECISION MAKING

Students use critical thinking skills to plan and conduct research, manage projects, solve problems and make informed decisions using appropriate digital tools and resources. Students:

  a. identify and define authentic problems and significant questions for investigation.

  b. plan and manage activities to develop a solution or complete a project.

  c. collect and analyze data to identify solutions and/or make informed decisions.

  d. use multiple processes and diverse perspectives to explore alternative solutions.

5. DIGITAL CITIZENSHIP

Students understand human, cultural, and societal issues related to technology and practice legal and ethical behavior. Students:

  a. advocate and practice safe, legal, and responsible use of information and technology.

  b. exhibit a positive attitude toward using technology that supports collaboration, learning, and productivity.

   c.   demonstrate personal responsibility for lifelong learning.

   d.   exhibit leadership for digital citizenship.

6. TECHNOLOGY OPERATIONS AND CONCEPTS

Students demonstrate a sound understanding of technology concepts, systems, and operations. Students:

   a.   understand and use technology systems.

   b.   select and use applications effectively and productively.

   c.   troubleshoot systems and applications.

   d.   transfer current knowledge to learning of new technologies.

APPENDIX C

Reading Group Guide

QUESTIONS FOR DISCUSSION

Chapter 1: Mapping the Journey—Seeing the Big Picture

The authors suggest that you use this book as a field guide to accompany you on a learning journey. What's motivating you to take this trip? What's prompting you to consider new approaches for teaching and learning? Imagine your most desirable fellow travelers. What do you have in common? Spend some time getting acquainted as a reading group. Compare your previous experiences with project-based learning.

Chapter 2: Creating a Professional Learning Community

Early in the chapter, Jeff Whipple makes this comment: "If I could do one thing for teachers to make school better for students, I'd find a way to have teachers have more time to work with each other and to develop collaborative projects." What connections do you see between teacher collaboration and student learning? Where do you find opportunities to collaborate with colleagues, both formally and informally? Can you imagine how you could bring more collaboration into your teaching life? Who would you include in your "dream team" for collaboration? Are you using technology to help you meet and connect with like-minded peers?

Chapter 3: Imagining the Possibilities

As you start to envision a digital-age project, which "big ideas" are you considering? How have you attempted to reach those same ideas before, with more traditional teaching? What do you expect to be different if you use the project approach? In this chapter, the authors suggest that "project learning, like real life, gets messy and overlaps multiple disciplines. It's in this overlapping space where great projects are born." Do you agree? As a group, review the Technology Focus: Essential Learning with Digital Tools, the Internet, and Web 2.0. Does this help frame your thinking about how to connect technologies with learning goals? What other technologies would you suggest using to accomplish any of these functions?

Chapter 4: Strategies for Discovery

Have you encountered any of the "project pitfalls" described in this chapter? What did you learn from your experience? Take a look at the list, "Where Project Ideas Come From." Have any of these been an inspiration for your own instructional planning? At the end of this chapter, the authors walk though a project design process. They suggest: "Strive for 'optimal ambiguity'—that is, both enough structure and enough flexibility to serve the needs of the project." What does "optimal ambiguity" mean to you? How do you imagine your learners responding to a project that is both structured *and* flexible?

Chapter 5: Project Management Strategies for Teachers and Learners

Project management skills include time management, communication, collaboration, effective use of resources, and troubleshooting. Where are your students most in need of specific skill building? How do you know? The authors suggest you will use multiple assessment methods during a project. Which assessment methods are you already using? How are you encouraging students to assess their own progress? The Technology Focus: Project Management with Technology describes a variety of project management interfaces. Which features are most desirable to you? Why?

Chapter 6: Project Launch—Implementation Strategies

The authors suggest engaging your students in building scoring guides for a project. What are your experiences with developing rubrics with your students? This chapter recommends waiting to do a K-W-L activity with your students until you have established interest and readiness to launch a project. How does this compare to your usual approach? Teacher Vicki Davis compares learning with the project approach to learning to drive. ("You would never put a beginner out on the interstate.") How do you imagine building your students' foundation skills so that they can be successful with projects?

Chapter 7: A Guiding Hand—Keeping a Project Moving

This chapter acknowledges "the art of teaching." What does this expression mean to you? In a project classroom, many kinds of conversations are taking place. What strategies do you use to make classroom discourse more productive? What do you learn from student-to-student dialogue? At times, teamwork can increase the potential for misunderstanding or conflict. Anne Davis's story shows how classroom conversation can be an essential troubleshooting strategy. She tells her students, "I need you to talk to me." How do you ensure that your students are comfortable sharing their challenges or setbacks?

Chapter 8: Building Connections and Branching Out

Digital tools enable students to connect with experts who may be geographically distant from their school. How might you prepare students *and experts* to make the most of these learning opportunities? The Flat Classroom Project catapulted two schools into the international limelight. Can you imagine how your students would react to this kind of "buzz"? The Spotlight: EAST Initiative Model outlines four key ideas that support rigorous, community-based learning. If these ideas became part of the culture of your current learning environment, how would the student experience change?

Chapter 9: Making Assessment Meaningful

Elise Mueller talks to her students about being "consumers or producers." Which role would your students say is more familiar to them? The authors pose this question: "How will you measure the distance each student travels as a learner?" What strategies do you find most effective for addressing and communicating students' individual gains as learners?

Chapter 10: Celebrating and Reflecting

This chapter emphasizes student reflection as a valuable step in the learning process. Do you regularly make time for student reflection? How do you make sure reflection is meaningful for your students? Some technology tools—such as blogs or podcasts—are well-suited to capture reflection. Which tools have you encouraged students to use for this learning function?

Chapter 11: Bringing It Home

At the outset, this book set the stage for a learning journey. How has the "travel" changed you? What new ideas will you be taking forward? How will your students benefit from what you have learned?

APPENDIX D

Bibliography

American Library Association. (1989). *Presidential committee on information literacy: Final report.* Retrieved July 22, 2007, from www.ala.org/ala/acrl/acrlpubs/whitepapers/presidential .htm

Anderson, L. W., & Krathwohl, D. R. (Eds.). (2001). *A taxonomy for learning, teaching, and assessing: A revision of Bloom's taxonomy of educational objectives.* New York: Longman.

Bill & Melinda Gates Foundation. (2005). *High schools for the new millennium: Imagine the possibilities.* Retrieved July 22, 2007, from www.gatesfoundation.org/UnitedStates/Education/ TransformingHighSchools/

Black, P., & Wiliam, D. (1998). Inside the black box: Raising standards through classroom assessment. *Phi Delta Kappan, 80*(2), 139–148. Retrieved July 22, 2007, from www.pdkintl.org/ kappan/kbla9810.htm

Boss, S. (n.d.) Finding the meaning: story 351. *Intel Education: An innovation odyssey.* Retrieved August 22, 2007, from www97.intel.com/odyssey/Story.aspx?storyid=351

Boss, S. (n.d.) *Highlights from Intel ISEF 2003.* Retrieved August 22, 2007, from page 8 at http:// download.intel.com/education/isef/2003Highlights.pdf

Boss, S. (n.d.) Students at the center: story 380. *Intel education: An innovation odyssey.* Retrieved August 22, 2007, from www97.intel.com/odyssey/Story.aspx?storyid=380

Boss, S. (n.d.) Thinking critically: story 332. *Intel education: An innovation odyssey.* Retrieved August 22, 2007, from http://educate.intel.com/odyssey/Story.aspx?storyid=332

Bridges, L. (1996). *Assessment: Continuous learning.* Portland, ME: Stenhouse.

Chard, S. (2007). *The project approach.* Retrieved July 22, 2007, from www.projectapproach.org

Claxton, G. (2003, October 10). Fit for life. *Times Educational Supplement.* Retrieved July 22, 2007, from www.tes.co.uk/section/story/?section=Archive&sub_section=Extras+%26+updates& story_id=385046&Type=0

Cotton, K. (2001). Classroom questioning. *Northwest Regional Educational Laboratory School Improvement Research Series,* 5. Retrieved July 22, 2007, from www.nwrel.org/scpd/sirs/3/ cu5.html

Darling-Hammond, L. (1994, Summer). Reinventing our schools: A conversation with Linda Darling-Hammond. *Technos Quarterly* 3(2). Retrieved August 2, 2007, from www.ait.net/technos/tq_03/2darling.php

Davis, A. (2007). *EduBlog insights*. Retrieved July 22, 2007, from http://anne.teachesme.com

Davis, V. (2006, Aug. 24). How I use wikis. What do you do? *Cool Cat Teacher Blog*. Retrieved July 22, 2007, from http://coolcatteacher.blogspot.com/2006_08_01_archive.html

Davis, V. (2006, Nov. 27). The classroom is flat: Teacherpreneurs and the flat classroom project kickoff. *Cool Cat Teacher Blog*. Retrieved July 22, 2007, from http://coolcatteacher.blogspot.com/2006_11_01_archive.html

Downtown Aurora Visual Arts. (n.d.). *Digital stories: The power of word*. Retrieved July 22, 2007, from www.davarts.org/art_storiesB.html

DuFour, R. (2004, May). Schools as learning communities. *Educational Leadership, 61*(8): 6–11.

DuFour, R., & Eaker, R. (1998). *Professional learning communities at work: Best practices for enhancing student achievement*. Bloomington, IN: National Educational Service.

Eaker, R., DuFour, R., & DuFour, R. (2002). *Getting started: Reculturing schools to become professional learning communities*. Bloomington, IN: National Educational Service.

Fagg, D. (2007). *iHistory podcast project*. Retrieved July 22, 2007, from http://ihistory.wordpress.com/2007/03

Hartley, L. (2007). *Classroom displays*. Retrieved July 22, 2007, from http://lmhartley.edublogs.org

Hord, S. M. (1997). *Professional learning communities: Communities of continuous inquiry and improvement*. Austin, TX: Southwest Educational Development Laboratory.

Kinory, A. (2003). *"Film at 11!" – iMovie™ makes essays come alive*. Retrieved August 26, 2007, from http://newali.apple.com/ali_sites/deli/exhibits/1000751/Introduction.html

Krauss, J. (1998). On project learning. *Northwest Regional Educational Laboratory classrooms@work/tools@hand*. Retrieved July 22, 2007, from http://netc.org/classrooms@work/classrooms/jane/orientation/prolearning.html

LaMonica, M. (2006, Dec. 1) Futurist: To fix education, think Web 2.0. *CNET News*.

Retrieved July 22, 2007, from http://news.com.com/Futurist+To+fix+education%2C+think+Web+2.0/2100-1032_3-6140175.html

Lindsay, J. (2006, Nov. 28). While I was playing tennis, the world got flatter. *E-Learning Blog*. Retrieved July 22, 2007, from http://123elearning.blogspot.com/2006/11/while-i-was-playing-tennis-world-got.html

Marzano, R., Pickering, D., & Pollock, J. (2001). *Classroom instruction that works*. Alexandria, VA: Association for Supervision and Curriculum Development.

McGrath, D. (2002–03, December/January). Launching a PBL project. *Learning & Leading with Technology, 30*(4): 36–39.

North Central Regional Educational Laboratory. (2003). en*Gauge 21st century skills: Literacy in the digital age*. Naperville, IL: Author.

Partnership for 21st Century Skills. (2003). *Learning for the 21st century*. Retrieved July 22, 2007, from www.21stcenturyskills.org/index.php?option=com_content&task=view&id=29&Itemid=42

Samuels, D. (2007, May 22). New medium for an old master. *The Oregonian*. p. B1. Retrieved July 22, 2007, from www.oregonlive.com/news/oregonian/index.ssf?/base/news/117980 4315201750.xml&coll=7

Senge, P. (2004). *The fifth discipline*. New York, NY: Currency Doubleday.

Teacher uses technology education. (2006, Nov. 18). *Malaya Living*. Retrieved July 22, 2007, from www.malaya.com.ph/nov18/livi1.htm

UNESCO LAMP (Literacy Assessment and Monitoring Programme). (2004). *International planning report*. Montréal: UIS.

Utecht, J. (2006, Dec. 10). I hate to write but love to blog... why? *The Thinking Stick*. Retrieved July 22, 2007, from www.thethinkingstick.com/?p=387

Valenza, J. K. (2000, April 20). For the best answers, ask tough questions. *Philadelphia Inquirer: Philly Online*.

Weinshenker, D. (n.d.) *Digital stories: The power of word*. Downtown Aurora Visual Arts Web site. Retrieved July 31, 2007, from www.davarts.org/art_storiesB.html

ADDITIONAL READINGS

Freedman, T. (Ed.). (2006). *Coming of age: An introduction to the new World Wide Web*. Great Britain: Terry Freedman Ltd. Retrieved from http://fordlog.com/?p=98

Kretzman, J., & McKnight, J. (1993). *Building communities from the inside out: A path toward finding and mobilizing a community's assets*. Evanston, IL: Asset-Based Community Development Institute.

Lang, Q.C. (Ed.). (2006). *Engaging in project work*. Singapore: McGraw-Hill Education (Asia).

Markham, T., Larmer, J., & Ravitz, J. (2003). *Project-based learning handbook*. Second Edition. Oakland, CA: Wilsted and Taylor.

Richardson, W. (2006). *Blogs, wikis, podcasts, and other powerful web tools for classrooms*. Thousand Oaks, CA: Corwin Press.

Stigler, J., & Hiebert, J. (1999). *The teaching gap: Best ideas from the world's teachers for improving education in the classroom*. New York: The Free Press.

Stites, R. (1998). "Evaluation of Project-Based Learning." *The multimedia project: Project-based learning with multimedia*. Redwood City, CA: San Mateo County Office of Education. Retrieved from http://pblmm.k12.ca.us/PBLGuide/pblresch.htm

Thomas, J.W. (2000). *A review of research on project-based learning*. San Rafael, CA: Autodesk Foundation. Retrieved from www.bobpearlman.org/BestPractices/PBL_Research.pdf

Warlick, D. (2004). *Redefining literacy for the 21st century*. Worthington, OH: Linworth.

INDEX

Italic page number indicate material in tables or figures.

2¢ Worth, *13*
21st-century skills and project-based learning, 47–51, 55

Active Learning Practices for Schools, *64*
Adobe Acrobat Connect, 177
AltaVista Family Filter, 179
American Library Association, 51
American Memory Project, 110, 168
American School Library Association, 48
America's Story, 168
anchors, learning journey, 140
AN Hosting, 174
AOL@School, 179
Apple Learning Interchange, *116*
ASK for Kids, 55, 111, 179
assessment
    asking students what they learned in, 143
    contests and publications and, 144
    creating something new and, 143
    end-of-learning, 139–40
    formative, 81–82
    grades and, 141–42, *142*
    modeling real-world, 144
    reading group guide, 189
    rubrics, 83, 101
    tools, *17*, 81–84
Asset-Based Community Development Institute, 73
asset maps, *70–73*
Avant, Brandy, 4

Bangladesh, 29–30, *80*, 89, 130
benefits of project-based learning, 10, 20, 136–37
Berkowitz, Bob, 111
Beyond School blog, *137*
Big6, 111
Bill & Melinda Gates Foundation, *17*, 26, 27
biography assignments, 48
Black, Paul, 81
Blogger, 56, 86, 175, 181
Blogmeister, 56, 175, 181
blogs
    community building with, 55, *164*, 174–75
    edu, *13–14*, 24, 136, 181
    with elementary students, 34
    project management, 88–89, *91*
    reflection, 56, 96, 181
    team, 107
Blogs, Wikis, Podcasts, and Other Powerful Web Tools for Classrooms, 45
Bloom's Taxonomy of Educational Objectives, 47
BlueHost, 174

bookmarking, social, *21–23*, 55, 179
Bridges, Lois, 82
Brown, John Seely, 52
bubbl.us, 172
Buck Institute for Education, *24*, *64*
budgeting, 76
Burell, Clay, *137*
Burg, Jerome, *36–37*, 141–42
Burt, Steve, *105*

Camtasia Studio Screen Recorder and Video Editor, *105*
Cassidy, Kathy, 44, 129, 162
Cassidy, Tony, 172
celebrating projects, 154, *155*, 189
Center for Innovation in Engineering and Science Education (CIESE), 38, 168
Chard, Sylvia, 62
Charles N. Fortes Magnet Academy, 150
Citation Machine, 55, 180
citizenship, digital, 184–85
ClassBlogmeister, 181
Classroom 2.0, 33
classroom discussions, 114–17, *118–19*
Classroom Displays, *152–53*, 172
Claxton, Guy, 52
Coalition of Essential Schools Northwest, *116*
collaboration
    assessing one's readiness for, 29–30
    asset maps and, *70–73*
    locating people for, 34–35, *70–73*
    National Educational Technology Standards for Students, 183–85
    networks, integrated, 86–87
    online communities, *33–34*, 38–39, 55, *64*, 82–83, *137*
    professional learning community, 30–31, 38–39
    reading groups, *40*
    reviewing student work in, 145
    student, 16, *17*, 19–20, 29, 177
    teacher, 25, 161–62, *162*, 176–78
    technology tools, 26, 84–87, 176–78
communication
    National Educational Technology Standards for Students, 183
    by students, 132–33
    by teachers, 161–62
completion, project
    celebrations, 154, *155*
    reflection at, 147–48
    sharing insights at, 161–62
    springboarding to the next project, 149
    student work displays, 154

computers, portable, 166
conflict management, 117–18
connections
    with experts, 128–29
    learning community expansions and, 129–31, 189
    technology and making, 127–28
contests, 144, 162–63
Cool Cat Teacher, 13, 131
Cort, David, 137
craigslist, 76
Crane, Carmel, 31, 79, 120, 144
creativity and innovation, National Educational Technology Standards for Students, 183
critical thinking, problem solving, and decision-making, 184
Curtis, Paul, 15–18, 113, 118, 141

Dabble DB, 170
Darling-Hammond, Linda, 140
Davis, Anne
    blogs, 13, 34, 117, 122, 131, 161
    reflection, 159
    use of outside experts, 128, 143
Davis, Vicki, 188
    assessment, 131
    blog, 13, 162
    collaboration, 19, 29–30, 80–81
    on cultural awareness, 118
    reflection, 160
deadlines and milestones, 78–79
deep learning, 54, 107–10, 168–70
Del.ici.ous, 21–22, 23, 55, 179
design, project, 62–63, 64, 67–70
    asset maps, 70–73
    project sketches in, 69–70
Desire2Learn, 55
Digg, 21, 23
digital citizenship, National Educational Technology Standards for Students, 184–85
Digital Edge Learning Interchange, 3
digital storage devices, 167
discrepant events, 97–98
discussions, classroom, 114–17, 118–19
displays, student work, 154
dispositions, learning, 51–52
Domino, 86
Doteasy, 174
Dozier, Matt, 133–34
Dreamhost, 174
Drupal, 87, 88
Durham, Scott, 11, 12

EBSCO, 110–11
echo effects of projects, 137
editing software, 3
EduBlog, 13, 56, 175
    Awards, 163
edubloggers, 13–14, 24, 34, 136, 181
Education Week, 14
Edutopia, 24

Eisenberg, Mike, 111
Electronic Emissary, 176
e-mail, 54, 167
Engadget, 166, 182
Environmental and Spatial Technologies, 133–35
essential functions, learning, 54–56
    collaboration, 176–78
    community building, 173–76
    making things visible and discussable, 170–73
    project management, 180
    reflection and iteration, 180–82
    research, 178–80
    ubiquity, 54, 165–68
Estoque, Cecilia Mag-isa, 19, 77–78
events, discrepant, 97–98
experts, 77, 102, 105, 128–29, 176
extended benefits of projects, 136–37

Fagg, David
    podcasts, 116, 118–19, 121, 122
    on reflection, 117, 118–19, 143, 148
feedback, 95
    just-in-time, 82–83, 103
    screencasting and, 104
FeedBurner, 176
field trips, virtual, 77
Fifth Discipline, The, 30
films, 3
filters, Internet, 179
Finland, 59
Flat Classroom Project
    assessment, 141, 144
    blog, 162
    fundamental skills taught before beginning, 100
    podcasting, 19, 122
    student collaboration, 130, 137
    team planning, 29–30, 80–81
    wiki, 89–90
Flat Stanley, 38
Flickr, 38, 54, 55, 86, 151–53, 172
folksonomy, 22, 172
Ford, Peter, 14
FordLog, the, 14
formative assessment, 81–82
Framework for 21st-Century Learning, 49
FreeMind Mindmapper, 54
Friedman, Thomas, 19, 130
Fryer, Wesley, 14, 122
Furl, 21, 23

George Lucas Educational Foundation, 24
Gizmo, 178
Gizmodo, 182
Global Cooling Collective, 137
Global Education Collaborative, 33
Global Information Systems, 132
Global Learning and Observations to Benefit the Environment (GLOBE), 38
global positioning devices, 54, 132, 133–35, 166
Global SchoolNet, 38–39, 60

Gmail, 167
Google Docs, 54, *74*, 82–83, 167, 169, 178
Google Earth, 21, *36–37*, 54, 98, 170
Google Lit Trips, *36–37, 37*
Google Maps, 171
Google Page Creator, 174
Google SafeSearch, 179
Google SketchUp, 172
GoToMeeting, 177
grades, 141–42, *142*
    See also assessment
Graham, Kay, 100
Granada High School, *36–37*
grants, technology, 26, 27, *27–28*
Grapes of Wrath, The, *36–37*
Griffin, Robert, 45, 66, 144

Hartley, Linda, *152–53*
Hewlett Packard Technology for Teaching Grants, 26
higher-order questions, 115–16
Human Genetics Project, the, 38

identity, school, 150–51
iGoogle, 56, 86, 180
iHistory Podcast, Australia, 116, 118–19, 121, *122*, 143, 148
Illuminations, 173
implementation, project
    assessment rubrics and, 101
    generating interest and promoting inquiry, 97–99
    laying groundwork for, 95–96
    reading group guide, 188
    setting the stage for independent inquiry, 100–101
    students' prior knowledge and, 96–97
    teaching fundamentals first, 100–101
    technology and, 3–6, 98–99, 101–2
    See also projects
independent inquiry, 100–101
Infoplease, 179
Inherit the Wind, 3
inquiry, promoting, 107–10, 117
insights, sharing teacher, 161–62
inspiration for projects, 65–66
instant messaging, 167
integrated collaboration networks, 86–87
Intel Education's Assessing Projects tool, 83
Intercultural E-mail Classroom Connections (IECC), 39, 177
International Boiling Point Project, 38
International Children's Digital Library, 179
International Education and Research Network (iEARN), 39, 60
Internet, the, 3
    blogs, *13–14, 24,* 34, 55, 56, 89, *91,* 136, *164,* 174–75
    bookmarking tools, *21–23, 179*
    classroom videos, *116*
    filters, 179
    Google Lit Trips, *36–37*
    locating free materials using, 76
    maps, 170–71

MySpace, *51,* 55, 173
online communities, *33–34,* 38–39, *51,* 55, *64,* 76, 79, 82–83, *131, 137, 164,* 173–76
    tracking assets using, 73–74
    personalized web pages, 89–91
    photo sharing, 37, 54, 55, 86, *151–53,* 172
    primary sources, 168
    project management on, 55–56, 79, 89–91
    real-time data, 168–69, *169–70*
    safe and robust searching, 111, 179
    tools for using data, 169–70
    tracking assets on, 73–74
    virtual manipulatives and modeling software, 173
    webcams, 171–72
    webinars, 55, 97, 177
    wikis, *45,* 56, *56–57,* 88, 89, *91,* 130, 149, 178, 181–82
    wireless, 166
IShowU, *105*
iteration and reflection, 56, 180–82

journals, project, 103
Journey North, 39

Kayuda, 172
KidsClick, 111, 179
Kid Zone, 170
Kinory, Adam, 3–5, 7, 103
Know-Wonder-Learn (K-W-L) activities, 96, 98, 100–101

Langhorst, Eric, 116
Laughing Squid, 174
Lazybase, 170
learning
    anchors, 140
    celebrating, 154
    communities, 129–31
    deep, 54, 107–10, 168–70
    dispositions, 51–52
    essential functions, 54–56, 165–82
    making things visible and discussible for, 54
    organizations, schools as, 30–31
    passion-based, 52
    reflection and iteration, 56
    themes, 61
    ubiquity, 54
    See also project-based learning
learning management systems (LMS), 86–87
Learning-Space, *84*
Lifehacker, 182
lifespans, project, 136–37
Lindsay, Julie, 19, 130–31
    blog, 162
    collaboration, 29
    reflection, 160, 163
    on team planning, *80–81*
LiveJournal, 181
logs, project, 103
Lotus Notes, *84*
Lycos Adult Content Filter, 179

management, project, 180
assessment planning, 81–84
    budgeting and, 76
    conflict management and, 117–18
    digital tools, 180
    gathering resources and, 76–78
    logs and journals, 103
    milestones and deadlines, 78–79
    online, 55–56, 79
    personalized web pages and, 89–91
    reading group guide, 188
    team planning, 79–80, 80–81
    with technology, 84–87
    web-based, 89–91
    wikis, 89
Mapping Community Assets Workbook, 73
MapQuest, 171
maps, 170–71
Marzano, Robert, 98
Mattila, Pasi, 59
McDowell, Michael, 15
    assessments, 84
    on questioning, 116
    reflection, 159, 163
    on team planning, 80
    on troubleshooting, 117
McGrath, Diane, 63
McIntosh, Ewan, *14*
McTighe, Jay, *64*
MediaWiki, 182
meetings, virtual, 177
messaging, instant, 167
Microsoft Worldwide Innovative Teachers Forum,
    162–63
milestones and deadlines, 78–79
mind mapping, 172
MindMeister, 172
mindomo, 172
mobile phones, 54, 59, 166
modeling software, 173
Montana Heritage Project, 136–37
Moodle, 56
Morbidity and Mortality Weekly Report, 169
Moveable Type, 181
Moving at the Speed of Creativity, 14, 122
MP3 players, 54, 166
MSN Hotmail, 167
Mueller, Elise, 139, 149
    on letting students lead, 136, 189
    professional learning community, *27–28*
    reflection, 159, 163
Myers, Bill, *105*
MySpace, *51,* 55, 173
My Yahoo!, 56, 86, 180

National Archives Educators and Students, 168
National Center for Research on Evaluation, Standards,
    and Student Testing, 139
National Educational Technology Standards for Stu-
    dents, 15, *24,* 26, 49

communication and collaboration, 183
    creativity and innovation, 183
    critical thinking, problem solving and decision-
        making, 184
    digital citizenship, 184–85
    research and information fluency, 184
    technology operations and concepts, 185
National Library of Virtual Manipulatives, 173
National Public Radio, 4
NetVibes, 54, 56, 86, 89–90, 167, 180
New Technology Foundation, 141
New Technology High School, 13
    online work, 79, 85–86
    structure, *15–18*
    student teams, 79–80, 117–18
    technology used by, 115
New York Times, 63
Noonday Project, the, 38

Oceanweather.inc, 169
Office 2.0 Database, 182
online communities, 79, *164*
    building, 173–76
    collaboration, *33–34,* 38–39, 55, *64, 82–83, 131,*
        137
    for free materials, 76
    MySpace, *51,* 55
    tracking assets using, *73–74*
OnStar, 132

Pageflakes, 86, 180
parents misconceptions about technology, 19
Partnership for 21st-Century Skills, 49
passion-based learning, 52
Pavlica, Robert, 129
PBwiki, 56, *56,* 182
PDAs, 54
peer review, 31
Philippines, the, 19, 77–78
photo sharing, 37, 54, 55, 86, *151–53,* 172
Picasa, 172
planning, team, 79–80, *80–81*
podcasting, 115, 116, 119–21, *121–22,* 130
Pogue, David, 166
portable computing devices, 166
Postman, Andrew, 63
preparation for project-based learning, 18–20
professional learning communities
    benefits of, 33
    collaboration, 30–31, 38–39
    creating, 30–31
    members, 34–35
    online, *33–34,* 38–39
    project-based learning collaboration as, 32–33
    reading group guide, 187–90
    reviewing student work together, *145*
    technology grants and, *27–28*
ProfilerPRO, 96
project-based learning
    assessment planning, 81–84

benefits of, 10, 20, 136–37
"big idea" in, 44–47
biography assignment, 48
Bloom's Taxonomy and, 47
budgeting, 76
collaboration in, 38–39, 70–73
enhancing curriculum, 43–44
gathering resources for, 76–78
getting ready for, 18–20
grants for, 27–28
led by students, 136
milestones and deadlines, 78–79
overlapping multiple disciplines in, 46–47
project management, 55–56, 180
promoting inquiry and deep learning, 107–10
21st-century skills and, 47–51, 55
successful, 12–13
teacher investment in, 20–21
team planning, 79–80, 80–81
technology in, 6, 11, 27–28, 53, 115–16
traditional, 12, 61
See also implementation, project; learning; projects
Project-Based Learning Online, 24
Project-Based Learning with Technology, 63
projects
applied to new contexts, 143
assessment rubrics, 83, 101
asset maps, 70–73
celebrating, 154, 155
communicating findings of, 132–33
design, 62–63, 64, 67–70
echo effect of, 137
entered in contests or submitted for publication, 144, 162–63
extended benefits of, 136–37
features of effective, 64–65
flexibility in, 62, 113–14
inspiration for, 65–66
lifespans, 136–37
photo sharing, 151–53
potential pitfalls of, 60–62
reviewing, 60
sketches, 69–70
springboarding to subsequent, 149, 159
troubleshooting, 116–17
See also implementation, project
Protopage, 56, 86, 89, 90, 167, 180
Public 911, 171
publication submissions, 144, 162–63

questions
for checking with students, 118–19
classroom discussion, 114–16, 114–17, 116
higher-order, 115–16
inquiry, 108–10, 117
reflection, 148

Radio Meteors, 169
reading groups, 40, 187–90
real-time data, 168–69, 169–70

reflection
blogs, 56, 96, 180–82
iteration and, 56, 180–82
at project end, 147–48, 189
questions, 148
student, 103, 147–48
wikis, 181–82
year in review, 154
Repositories of Primary Sources, 168
research and information fluency, National Educational Technology Standards for Students, 184
resources, gathering, 76–78
Richardson, Will, 14, 34, 45, 104, 117
role-playing, 97
RSS feeds, 86
Rubistar, 83
rubrics, scoring, 83, 101
Russo, Alexander, 14

Santa Fe Indian School, 132
School and Community Reuse Action Project, 76
school identity, 150–51
School of the Future, 7
Schools of California Online Resources for Education (SCORE), 169
scoring rubrics, 83, 101
Scotland, 13
screencasting, 104–6
search engines, 111, 179
Senge, Peter, 30
Shakespeare Explorer, 171
Singapore, 13
Site 5, 174
sketches, project, 69–70
Skype, 86, 130, 178
slideshows, 104
social bookmarking, 21–23, 55, 179
Square of Life, the, 38
Stephenson, Tim, 134
students
blogs, 174–75
classroom discussions, 114–17
collaboration, 16, 17, 19–20, 29, 177
communicating their finding, 132–33
familiarity with digital technology, 6, 46, 102–3
feedback for, 82–83, 95, 103
leading their own projects, 136
living and learning in the real world, 6
MySpace and, 51, 55, 173
personalized web pages, 89–91
point of view, 52–53
questions for checking in with, 118–19
reflection by, 103, 147–48
safe and robust Internet searching by, 111, 179
school identity and, 150–51
self-evaluation by, 95
teaching other students, 102–3
teams, 79–80
work displays, 154
submissions, publication, 144, 162–63
SurveyMonkey, 73, 96

Index

Tapped In, *34*
Teach Digital: Curriculum, 122
    teachers
    classroom discussions, 114–17
    collaboration, 25, 161, 162, 176–78
    implementation of technology by, 3–6
    investment in project-based learning, 20–21
    just-in-time feedback, *82–83*
    as learners, 14–15
    online communities, *33–34, 38–39, 64, 164*
    peer review, 31
    readiness for teamwork, 29–30
    sharing insights, 161–62
    wikis, 56–57
TechCrunch, 166, 182
technology
    collaboration and, 26, *84–87*, 176–78
    demonstrating, 103
    experts, *105*, 106
    grants, 26, 27–28
    literacy and Big6, 111
    National Educational Technology Standards for
        Students, 185
    optimizing, 115–16
    parents' misconceptions about, 19
    preparing to use, 101–2
    in project-based learning, 6, 11, 27–28, 53
    project implementation and, 98–99, 101–2
    project management with, *84–87*
    resources, 76–78
    screencasting, *104–6*
    specialists, *105*, 106
    21st-century skills and, 47–51
    use by students, 6, 46, 102
Textpattern, 87
themes, 61
Thinking Stick, the, *14*, 136
Thinkmap Visual Thesaurus, 54, 171
Timber Drive Elementary School, 102
Tipton, Monica, *16, 17, 18*
troubleshooting, 116–17
Tulalip Elementary School, 137

U.S. Geological Survey, 169
ubiquity, 54, 165–68
Udell, Jon, *105*
Understanding by Design, *64*
United Nations Cyber School Bus, 110
United Nations Educational, Scientific, and Cultural
        Organization (UNESCO), 49
United States Geological Survey, 110
Utecht, Jeff, *14*, 136

Valenza, Joyce, 108
video cameras, 3, 171–72
videoconferencing, 77
virtual field trips, 77
virtual manipulatives, 173
virtual meetings, 177
Virtual Reference Desk AskA Service, 176
voice-over IP calling, 86, 178

Warlick, David, *13*, 50, 180
Web-based Inquiry Science Environment
        (WISE), 39
webcams, 171–72
WebEx, 177
Webinars, 55, 97, 177
Weblogg-ed, *14*
Web mail, 54, 167
Web sites, 173–74
Week in Education, *14*
Weighill, Cheryl, 62–63
Weinshenker, Daniel, 127
WhaleNet Active Satellite Tags, 169
Whipple, Jeff, 25, 29, 50, 130, 187
Wi-Fi, 166
Wiggins, Grant, *64*
wikis, *45*, 130, 178
    for grant writing, 149
    project management using, 56, *56–57*, 89, *91*
    reflection using, 181–82
Wikispaces, 56, 182
William, Dylan, 81
WiMax, 166
Windows Live Spaces, 181
wireless internet, 166
Wise Up, 52
Wojcicki, Esther, *82–83*
Wordpress, 174, 175, 181
World Factbook, 168
World is Flat, The, 19, 29, 86, 130
Worldometers, 169
World Wide Web, the. *See* Internet, the

Yahoo! Kids, 111
Yahoo! Mail, 167
Yahoo! Maps, 171
Yahoo SafeSearch, 179
Yahoo! Web Hosting, 174
YouTube, 3, *116*

Zelinka, Koty, *50–51*
Zoho Creator, *74*, 170, 178
Zoho Virtual Office, 167, 169
Zoomerang, 96